THE ETERNAL WOMAN

Gertrud von le Fort

THE ETERNAL WOMAN

THE WOMAN IN TIME

TIMELESS WOMAN

TRANSLATED FROM THE LATEST
REVISED GERMAN EDITION WITH A
PREFACE BY PLACID JORDAN, O.S.B.

THE BRUCE PUBLISHING COMPANY
MILWAUKEE

301
✓

IMPRIMI POTEST:
      BENEDICTUS REETZ, O.S.B.
      Archiabbas Beuronensis

NIHIL OBSTAT:
      JOHN A. SCHULIEN, S.T.D.
      Censor librorum

IMPRIMATUR:
      ✠ WILLIAM E. COUSINS
      Archbishop of Milwaukee

      August 31, 1961

Library of Congress Catalog Card Number: 62-11029

© 1962 THE BRUCE PUBLISHING COMPANY
MADE IN THE UNITED STATES OF AMERICA

PREFACE

This book was first published in Germany, in 1934. At this writing, over one hundred thousand copies of the German original have been sold, and so far the book has been translated into French, Italian, Spanish, Portuguese, and Dutch. All these translations have been difficult to provide, for the German version itself is not easy reading, and translating it in each instance has constituted a task requiring unusual skill.

Various attempts had been made in the English language. Excerpts of the book first became available to American readers in the *Commonweal*, New York, in 1936. This full English translation represents the best efforts of both translator and publisher to produce a classic in its own right. It incorporates the revisions and additions of the latest German printing.

It can be said without fear of contradiction that no book like this has ever before been written, none certainly as penetrating and with as deep an insight into this difficult subject. It is a book on Woman written by a woman whose competence in dealing with her topic is unique. For Gertrud von le Fort is not only a trained philosopher and historian, but also a highly gifted poet and, above all, steeped in the noblest traditions of the Christian past, which in the light of the present day she interprets with rare mastery.

Her biography is brief. Born on October 11, 1876, at Minden, Westphalia, she hails from a family of French origin. Her forebears in Savoy first emigrated to Italy in the sixteenth century and then settled in Geneva, Switzerland, but later generations moved on to Russia and eventually to Germany. Baroness von le Fort could not have wished for an education more enlightening than the history of her own family, which reflects nearly every facet of Europe's cultural and religious heritage.

Surrounded by a typically Protestant atmosphere, she spent a happy youth on her family's estate of Boek on Lake Mueritz in Mecklenburg. Her father, Baron Lothar von le Fort, was an officer of the Prussian army, carrying on, at it were, from where his ancestors in France had left off when they served in the armies of Louis XVI. Her mother, Elsbeth, nee von Wedel-Parlow, was also of aristocratic lineage. In a small volume incorporating some of her memoirs Gertrud von le Fort has written of her parents with deep affection. After a happy and carefree childhood she enjoyed a private education at home and then attended a Hildesheim girls' college. After her graduation she enrolled at Heidelberg University.

At Heidelberg, and at the Universities of Berlin and Marburg, she dedicated herself for several years to both historical and philosophical studies which, combined with travel, especially in Italy, helped her gain an appreciation of things Catholic. After the death of her parents she moved to Baierbrunn near Munich in the company of one of her sisters, and in 1926 became a convert to the Catholic faith. She was received into the fold of the Church Universal in Santa Maria dell'Anima, the German parish church of Rome. Since the end of World War II she has resided at Oberstdorf in the Bavarian Alps. Now in her eighty-sixth year of age, but still of youthful temperament and vigorous in spirit, she continues to be actively engaged in her writing. Recently she was awarded the Annette von Droste Prize in Literature, the Poetry Prize of North Rhine Westphalia, the Munich Poetry Prize in Germany, and the Gottfried Keller citation of Switzerland. She is also a member of the Academy of the Gallery of Living Catholic Authors, of Webster Groves, Mo. The University of Munich has conferred upon her an honorary doctorate of Catholic theology — a rare distinction indeed.

Gertrud von le Fort was first attracted to the Catholic

Church as a young girl while visiting in the Rhineland. These impressions were deepened during her stay at the Hildesheim College, but did not really mature until she had the opportunity of a protracted residence in the Eternal City. Her superb first novel, *The Veil of Veronica* (which Sheed and Ward published in an English translation), reflected her Roman experiences. Eventually they led to her conversion. Her truly magnificent *Hymns to the Church*, beautifully translated into English by Mary Chanler (another Sheed and Ward publication), heralded this decisive event of her life.

Since then Gertrud von le Fort has been a prolific writer who has gained prominence not only in Germany, but throughout Europe. Besides the two books mentioned, only her masterful novels *The Song at the Scaffold* and *The Pope From the Ghetto* are available in English. Some thirty additional volumes, most of them poetry and novels, await translation. It is fervently to be hoped that some day these writings will all become accessible to the English-speaking world. They are on a level with those of the greatest Catholic and non-Catholic writers of this age and often reach the excellence of classics that will endure.

*　　*　　*

Gertrud von le Fort's message is drawn from the main spring of Christian revelation. Her basic theme is that strength which according to St. Paul "is made perfect in weakness" (2 Cor. 12:9). Strength in weakness, in a power-drunk, secularized world bristling with arms and at the same time bleeding from a million wounds because man, both physically and mentally, has run amuck.

In *The Song at the Scaffold*, Blanche de la Force, the young Carmelite novice, is portrayed as holding the likeness of the Christ Child in her arms. "So small and so weak," she says. But Sister Marie of the Incarnation replies: "No, so small and so powerful." Even more cogently Sister Marie adds a little later that "to tremble is to be strong," for in trembling we realize, as does fearful little Blanche, the very moment she is trampled to death by an infuriated crowd of revolutionists, "the infinite frailty of our vaunted powers."

In *The Wedding of Magdeburg*, an historical novel dealing with an episode in the Thirty Years' War, Gertrud von le Fort, in a breath-taking sentence, has thrown down the gauntlet to all the believers in a merely material progress, to all the worldly perfectionists and superficial rationalists. "Christ," she says, "does not emerge in a struggle *against* the Cross, but on the Cross — just as love always is triumphant in surrender." This leitmotif recurs throughout her writings to make us realize the paradox of Christian truth by the standards of eternal life. Seeming defeat ending in conquest, supreme sacrifice in triumph, crucifixion in resurrection — against the backdrop of historic scenes this appears as the fruit of all human experience, if we but tremble in the strength of Christ.

Perhaps the realization that man's weakness is his real and only strength, his surrender to God's holy will the only true victory he can achieve, perhaps such an awareness is more connate to feminine than to masculine nature. Of course, we must understand these terms properly as spiritual principles and polar forces which can find expression in both man and woman. In both there can be pride, and both can be children of Mary as true handmaids of the Lord. It is from this premise that Gertrud von le Fort has developed her profound metaphysical interpretation of womanhood. The eternal femininity as a theological mystery is the subject matter of this book on *The Eternal Woman*, which in her own words deals with "the religious significance of femininity and its ultimate reflection in God."

Again we must remember what St. Paul says about strength being made perfect in weakness or, as some translators render the passage more aptly, power revealing itself in infirmity. Power and strength ultimately are not of this world, but of the kingdom of God. There is only one way to achieve it: by surrendering to God's will. To use Gertrud von le Fort's own words: "Surrender to God is the only absolute power with which the creature is endowed." And again: "To bring about his salvation, all man has to contribute is his readiness to give himself up completely. The receptive, passive attitude of the feminine principle appears as the decisive, the positive element in the Christian order of grace. The Marian dogma, brought down to a simple formula, means the co-operation of the creature in the salvation of the world."

Mary's fiat, then, her willingness to let God's will be done, appears as the power in her infirmity. In woman's constitutive desire to surrender, to give herself, rests the very depth of life, for such surrender is the expression of the creature's unquestioning acceptance of the will of God. That is why Gertrud von le Fort says pointedly that "the world can be moved by the strength of man, but it can be blessed, in the real sense of the word, only in the sign of woman."

In her novel *The Child's Kingdom*, which represents the introduction to a medieval trilogy not yet completed, Gertrud von le Fort has clearly indicated the sequence she has in mind. "First," she says, "comes creation which is the glory of God, then comes conception which is the humility of woman, and only then comes action which is the power of man." The implication is obvious that there can be no action, no "masculine" activity in life without the "conception" of divine grace preceding it. Gertrud von le Fort throws further light on her reasoning when she goes on to say that "the hour preceding all creation is not called our power, but our helplessness — which is the only omnipotence . . . ," for by surrendering, the creature becomes co-powerful with the Creator. All the achievements of man depend on this primary act of creative surrender which leads to a divine partnership. Did not Christ Himself tell Pilate that he would have no power unless it were given him from above? (Jn. 19:11.)

The issue is fundamental and should be brought home to all those who are willing to meet the challenge of Christian thinking. What Gertrud von le Fort says as a Catholic, others have expressed just as convincingly from their various denominational perspectives. C. S. Lewis, for instance, when he wrote that "our role must always be that of patient to agent, female to male, mirror to light, echo to voice" (*The Problem of Pain*, page 39, Macmillan, 1944). The Anglican scholar proceeds to explain that our highest activity must be response, not initiative, because "our freedom is only a freedom to better or worse response." Nicholas Berdyaev, the late Russian philosopher, has reached conclusions along similar lines. "Within the sphere of humanity and in the natural world," he writes (*Freedom and the Spirit*, page 177, Scribner's, 1935), "there had to be a pure and spotless being capable of receiving the divine element, a feminine principle enlightened by grace." As one of the Greek Orthodox faith, he sees this being in Mary, the Mother of God. Her *fiat* was "the answering love of man to the infinite divine love."

Modern man finds it difficult to absorb such thoughts, for he has lost the sense of mystery. He tries to deny the mystery of life and to ignore its transcendental reality. Woman is as much lost in the resultant chaos and anarchy as man. She has given up her birthright, as it were, by discarding the veil, by forcing her way from the depth of life to the foreground of life. In this light we can well understand how the symbol of the veil became a pivotal element in Gertrud von le Fort's thinking. It is an eminently feminine symbol which indicates that woman is inaccessible in her innermost being when she becomes the mother of life, and birth is born out of her depth, in silence and solitude. "The unveiling of woman," says Gertrud von le Fort, "always means the breakdown of her mystery." And she quotes the words of another great contemporary poet of Germany, Ruth Schaumann: "It is always the mystery which bears fruit while what is patent, and revealed, is an end."

On woman, then, center the dominant issues of human history. Pride or surrender is the tremendous alternative. Clearly the struggle is not only one of our day, for the present is but

x

a mirror of the past. There is an almost straight line linking up the naturalistic and pragmatist philosophies which have weakened man's metaphysical outlook on life. The "age of reason" has led to an age of chaos. The schools of thought which made all values relative, or strictly secular and profane, developed of necessity an anarchic individualism which became the forerunner of modern paganism. Because it had become spiritually hollow and indifferent, the modern world apostatized morally and intellectually. Amidst carnivals of despair, man set up new idols, built new Towers of Babel, only to find himself lost in the mad whirl of demonic forces which now has assumed gigantic proportions.

Amidst this pitched battle between darkness and light it is woman's specific calling to restore the right balance which is a prerequisite of all stability. "Women," said Richard Cardinal Cushing of Boston in a recent address, "must restore to political and professional life the emphasis on the spiritual, an emphasis now so sadly lacking; we rely on them to help win the spiritual battle against the evils of secularism." Dare we hope that in an age which cheapens womanhood by primitive and inanely vulgar displays, such higher ideals will prevail? Has the trend run its course which started from the pretense that woman could make her best contribution toward human progress by being "equal" to man, rather than by being herself? If woman, both physically and spiritually, fails to exercise her specific function as mother of life, mankind faces a vacuum where her mystery ought to bear fruit. In the midst of anarchy and despair the right balance must be restored between the masculine and the feminine forces, and woman must assert her influence as a woman, by means of her healing, womanly power, to restore order to a derelict human race. This book is an invaluable contribution toward that end.

PLACID JORDAN, O.S.B.

Beuron, Benedictine Archabbey
Feast of the Immaculate Conception, 1961

INTRODUCTION

This book is an attempt to interpret the significance of woman, not in the light of her psychological or biological, her historical or social position, but under her symbolic aspect. This will imply a certain difficulty for the reader. The language of symbols, once universally understood as an expression of living thought, has largely been replaced today by the language of abstract thinking; in consequence, this book must assume the obligation of helping the reader understand the meaning of the symbol.

Symbols are signs or images we use as means to apprehend supreme metaphysical realities and truths, not in an abstract manner but by way of a likeness. Symbols, then, are the language of an invisible realm becoming tangible in the realm of the visible. This concept of the symbol springs from the conviction that in all creation there is a meaningful order revealing itself as divinely ordained by making use of the language of symbols.

The individual carrier, therefore, has an obligation toward his symbols. They remain above and beyond him, inviolate and inviolable, even when the individual no longer recognizes their meaning, or when he has gone so far as even to reject or deny them. For the symbol does not disclose the empirical character or condition of its respective bearer. Rather it expresses his metaphysical significance. The bearer may discard his symbol; but the symbol itself will remain.

Just as the meaning of the symbol does not necessarily coincide with the empirical character or condition of its respective bearer, so also the essential quality the symbol designates is not restricted to a given individual. We maintain that because of her symbol, woman has a special affiliation with the religious sphere. To conclude from this that woman is particularly religious, or even holds supremacy over man in this respect, would amount to a complete misunderstanding of this book. What we are concerned with is the figurative aspect of religious experience, its symbolic representation. This latter, however, we feel has been in a special measure entrusted to woman because of her very symbol.

What is true of the feminine principle in its fundamental significance applies also to the significance of its individual expressions. This book is concerned throughout with revelation as it comes through woman. Of course, this does not imply that such revelation belongs to woman only, in so far as its metaphysical reality is concerned; for here on earth the revelation of all being is a twofold one. This is precisely what the two forms of masculine life that are greatest in symbolic significance demonstrate. In the truly heroic manifestation of manhood the strong strain of womanly compassion appears, but under a masculine aspect, and the chivalrous man always protects the weak and helpless. Thus a St. Vincent de Paul, man and priest, takes the abandoned child of the stranger to his heart as a woman would. And thus in St. Aloysius Gonzaga, as well as in all typical figures of spiritual knighthood, virginity also becomes evident as a masculine virtue.

It is but a recognition of this twofold revelation of femininity, although under a different aspect, when St. Catherine of Siena upholds precisely the virile virtues as essential to the genuinely Christian life. It is also the supreme acknowledgment of this twofold manifestation when the Litany of Loreto, which is so deeply imbued with dogma, invokes Mary both as Mother most amiable and Virgin most powerful, and places the womanly image of the Mystical Rose beside the masculine symbols: Mirror of Justice and Tower of David. Like every truth concerning woman, this image of the Eternal Woman also leads to an understanding of the symbolic significance of womanliness. Mary, standing for the creature in its totality, represents at one and the same time both man and woman.

CONTENTS

THE ETERNAL WOMAN

THE ETERNAL WOMAN

Whenever a creature is seen under the aspect of eternity, our concern is no longer the creature itself, but the eternity of God, who alone is eternal. Only an age profoundly bewildered, one distracted from its metaphysical roots, could attribute the idea of eternity, be it regarded as absolute value or absolute duration, to mere creatures,[1] without realizing that such concepts, rather than exalting a person, amount to its annihilation. Referred to its eternal origin, the created being becomes aware of its own relativity, and only then does eternity acknowledge the creature.

Due to its limitations in time and its contingency upon the absolute realities, the creature is bound to be submerged when faced by timelessness and, thus absorbed, appears no longer as a value in itself, but as a thought or mirror of the eternal, as its symbol or vessel. This is the meaning of all purification, of every religious surrender; it is the meaning of saint and lover; it also is the meaning of death. In this sense only may we here venture to speak of the Eternal Woman. Therefore it is by no means a question of presenting or even of transposing certain characteristics of the empirical image of woman which are relatively unchanging and might, in a restricted, earthly sense, be termed eternal. It is rather a matter of the cosmic, the metaphysical countenance of woman; of womanliness as a mystery, its religious rank, its archetype and ultimate origin in God.

This obviously implies that every arbitrary attempt at interpretation must be rejected. Religious experience, as we have

---

[1] Translator's note: The allusion is clearly to certain political leaders of our day.

seen, begins where individual self-will is given up. But beyond this point, what language shall we speak? We cannot grasp the metaphysical reality except under the veil of tangible forms, which again confines us to the sphere of relative and passing values. Only great art in its supreme moments of inspiration is capable of expressing eternal concepts by ephemeral means.

As soon as we interrogate art, however, we are confronted by another revelation, namely, that our great occidental art can never be detached from Catholic dogma; that, under its eternal aspects, it actually has a priestly function. Just as Beethoven's mighty *Missa Solemnis* continues to attract to the Credo of the Church thousands upon thousands whom the Church itself can no longer reach, so also great painting and sculpture carry throughout the centuries, even down to the modern pagan, the victorious message of the Christian drama of Redemption. An inquiry into occidental art not only in its aesthetic but also in its religious content means, therefore, to tread the ground of great Catholic dogma whose foundation is not merely temporal and personal, and upon which rests the whole culture of the Western world. Even in denying Catholic dogma this culture is indissolubly bound to it as its very foundation.

Let us realize first of all that Catholic dogma has formulated the most powerful pronouncements ever made about woman. In the face of these, all other attempts at a metaphysical interpretation of womanhood vanish like a mere echo of theology, or as something senseless so far as the religious meaning is concerned. Not only has the Church in her teaching about the sacrament of matrimony compared woman, that is, every woman, to herself, but she has proclaimed a woman as Queen of Heaven; she has called her Mother of the Redeemer and Mother of Divine Grace.

By these expressions, of course, the Church did not have in mind the incarnation of womanliness as such. She referred only to the one who has been called "blessed among women." However, this blessed one, although she is immeasurably more than

2

the symbol of womanhood, is nevertheless also this very symbol; for, in her alone the metaphysical mystery of woman has become tangible and hence intelligible.

Let us try briefly to understand the content of the dogma. If we seek counsel from the great masters who depicted the life of Mary, Fra Angelico, for example, we must begin with the last painting of the series, for in reality it is the first. With intimations of a dogmatic evolution which then was still in progress, religious art of the past reflects in the order of these paintings the later unfolding of Catholic dogma, for only in the last picture, that of the Coronation of the Blessed Virgin, does the Immaculata become entirely visible. This dogma, historically considered, has been defined late; metaphysically, however, it stands at the beginning of the mystery, even at the beginning of all things, disappearing as it were into the morning glow of the first hour of creation.

The dogma of the Immaculate Conception means the revelation of what the human being was prior to the fall; it betokens the countenance of the creature before its desecration, the image of God in man. Under this perspective a unique light is thrown upon the circumstances in which the dogma was defined. For by the standards of the Church this definition occurred at the time, to use an expression of the Christian historian and philosopher Berdyaev,[2] of the "downfall of the human image," a coincidence, the full significance of which we can understand only today.

The tremendous and universal meaning of the Marian dogma becomes obvious in the light of these considerations. If the Immaculata is God's inviolate image of humanity, then the Virgin of the Annunciation is its representative. The mystery of the Redemption in so far as it depends upon the creature is predicated on the humble fiat of her answer to the angel.

---

[2] Nicholas Berdyaev (1874–1948), prominent Russian historian and philosopher. His books *The Meaning of History* and *The End of Our Time* are probably the best known of his many writings. He was a firm believer in Christianity and an adherent to its Russian Orthodox pattern.

For his redemption, man has nothing to contribute to God other than the readiness of unconditional surrender. The passive acceptance inherent in woman, which ancient philosophy regarded as purely negative, appears in the Christian order of grace as the positively decisive factor. The Marian dogma, reduced to a brief formula, expresses the co-operation of the creature in the work of salvation.

The *fiat* of the Virgin is therefore the revelation of the very essence of religious experience. Since, as an act of surrender, the *fiat* is at the same time an essential expression of womanliness, the latter becomes the manifestation of the religious element itself in human nature. Mary, then, is not only the object of religious veneration; but in her very being she reflects the religious nature of mankind which is at the bottom of all worship and in the form of the bridal woman symbolizes the power of surrender of all creation.

Among non-Catholics the veneration of Mary often is misunderstood because of the assumption that it involves making some sort of goddess of the Mother of God, when the very opposite is the truth. The invocation of Mary does not mean the invocation of a goddess. What is meant is a profession of faith in the sense of the willingness of man to surrender, which in turn signifies an understanding of the mystery of man's co-operation with God who alone is the source of all creation.[3]

It is this that the Litany of Loreto has in mind when, with the power of great poetry as well as of great dogma, it invokes Mary as the Morning Star, for the morning star rises in advance of the sun in order to lose its identity by disappearing in the light of the sun. In like manner the Divine Son at Mary's breast signifies, with regard to her, that she is submerged in His splendor. Only when so submerged is she the Mother of Divine Grace and in this sense only is she also the Mother of

---

[3] The Catholic Church does not accept the view of the total corruption of human nature by sin, but leaves to the fallen creature the extent to which it may be willing to co-operate with divine grace.

4

the Cross and of Sorrows. As the glory of her Son outshines her, so His death struggle overshadows her. In her sorrow too, she is not herself but the one who surrenders, the one who is suffering with her Son. But the one who suffers with Him is also the one who has a share in His work of Redemption. The term "co-redemption," so frequently misunderstood, means only the mother: Mother of the Redeemer, Mother of salvation.

Under this aspect the position of Mary in the history of Christianity becomes understandable. Seldom mentioned in the Gospels, overlooked over long stretches in the history of the Church, Mary's great dogmas invariably arise at junctures of gravest danger to the Christian Faith. The fundamental dogma concerning her was proclaimed at the Council of Ephesus and constitutes a part of the refutation of the Nestorian heresy in its bearings upon Christology.[4] Even in the dogma most intimately hers, Mary does not come into prominence for her own sake, but because of her Son. Her human personality in its psychological details is inaccessible to every historically critical analysis, to all merely intellectual interpretation, even to the most ardent love. For her likeness remains veiled, as it were, in the mystery of God.

It is veiled, however, for the express purpose of stressing its religious significance, for on earth the veil is the symbol of the metaphysical. It is also the symbol of womanhood, since all the important aspects of woman's life show her veiled. This makes it evident why the greatest mysteries of Christianity entered the created world not through the man, but by way of the woman. The annunciation of the Christmas message to Mary is repeated in the Easter message to Magdalen, while the mystery of Pentecost reveals man in an attitude of womanly receptivity. The Church indicates this same relevance when at religious services and also at the marriage ceremony she assigns woman to the gospel side of the altar.

---

[4] Nestorius maintained that there were two persons in Christ while the Church upholds the doctrine of one person in two natures.

5

In like manner woman's significance in a metaphysical sense becomes evident in the countenance of Mary inasmuch as the very cradle of the Church is intimately related to the concept of virginity. This is clearly indicated by the fact that the womb of a motherly woman was the first abode of Redemption on earth. The beautiful designation of the Church as a mother can be traced back to Mary.

Thus we see that surrender as a metaphysical mystery, as a mystery of Redemption, according to Catholic dogma is the mystery of woman rendered visible with unique perfection and surpassing that of every creature in the image of the Blessed Virgin and Mother, but duplicated, nay, multiplied a thousand times as in a tremendous hierarchy of surrender. As the Sibyl rises in advance of Mary, so the cosmic mystery precedes the Christian mystery of Redemption as though it were prophetic.

The motif of womanhood echoes through all creation. Like a far-off, tender prelude, it hovers above the opened womb of the bridal earth and broods over the fond mother beast of the wilds, which in its motherhood almost breaks its animal barriers. It is poised over the loving bride and wife, suspended in abounding measure over every human mother eclipsed in the radiance of her child. It is recognizable still in the sensuously prodigal mistress and lingers over the most trivial, the most transitory act of giving; upon the smallest, the most childlike kindness, even upon its faintest intimation. It ascends out of the natural sphere to that which is spiritual and supernatural. Wherever woman is most profoundly herself, she is so not as herself but as surrendered; and wherever she is surrendered, there she is also bride and mother. The nun dedicated to adoration, to works of mercy, to the mission field, carries the title of mother; she bears it as virgin mother. The sibyl who with "foaming lips" announces a new aeon is the mother of that which is to come, for all prophecy is but a form of motherhood. As the sibyl precedes Mary, so the saint succeeds her. In her the primal mystery returns to the place that is its home.

6

It is profoundly understandable, therefore, that the most astounding achievements of women have been connected with the sphere of religion. St. Catherine of Siena was entrusted with the task of bringing the Pope from Avignon back to Rome, and she did it. St. Joan of Arc even carried a banner on the battlefield. However, it is pre-eminently in the manner of a bride, that is, under a veil, that woman receives these extraordinary commitments. It is precisely the veil that is the evidence of every important womanly mission. For this reason St. Catherine of Siena was not present when the Pope returned to Rome and St. Joan received her veil in the flames of the funeral pyre.

In keeping with the veil motif, the unpretentious more than anything else belongs to the domain of woman, and this means all that belongs to love, goodness, compassion, everything that has to do with nursing and fostering the hidden, the betrayed things of the earth. Therefore, the times when woman is crowded out of public life are not in the least detrimental to her metaphysical significance. On the contrary, probably these very periods, for the most part unknowingly, throw the immense weight of womanhood into the scales of the world.

Whenever there is surrender, there also is a gleam from the mystery of the Eternal Woman, but when the woman seeks herself, her metaphysical mystery is extinguished; for in raising up her own image she destroys the image that is eternal. Only from this perspective does the great defection of the woman — that is, Eve — become understandable. To seek its meaning in the contradiction between the sensual and the spiritual would be a mistake. The defection of woman is not really a desertion of the creature; it is rather an apostasy away from the earth in so far as the earth itself signifies something womanly, something that awaits in humble readiness. The fall in the Paradise story is not contingent upon the temptation through the sweetness of the fruit, nor does it hinge upon the challenge to acquire the autonomous knowledge of good and evil; but it is the result of

7

the deceiving promise "You shall be like unto God," which is the contradiction to the *fiat* of the Virgin. The actual apostasy, therefore, occurs in the religious realm and consequently, in its deepest sense, signifies the fall of woman. This is not because Eve was the first to pick the fruit; but because she took it as woman. Creation fell in its womanly substance, for it fell in its religious aspect. The larger responsibility, therefore, in the Bible story is shouldered upon Eve, not upon Adam.

On the other hand, it is entirely wrong to say that Eve fell because she was the weaker. The Bible story shows clearly that she was the stronger and had the ascendancy over man. Man, regarded in his cosmic aspect, stands in the foreground of strength, while woman dwells in its deeper reaches. Whenever woman has been suppressed, it was never because she was weak, but because she was recognized and feared as having power; and this with good reason, for whenever the stronger power no longer desires surrender but seeks its own glory a catastrophe is bound to ensue. The atavistic tradition of the struggle that arose in the last phase of a mythical matriarchate still quivers with the fear of woman's power. For the opposite of the most profound surrender is the possibility of utter refusal, and this is the negative aspect of the metaphysical mystery of woman. Because in her very being, and in her innermost meaning, she is not only destined to surrender, but constitutes the very power of surrender that is in the cosmos, woman's refusal to surrender denotes something demoniacal and is readily experienced as such. While she is never the power of evil in itself — the fallen angel exceeds her in revolt and the devil is masculine — she shares the devil's power of seduction.

Seduction is self-will, the opposite to surrender. Since the fallen angel is more terrifying than the fallen human being, so also is the woman who falls more terrifying than the man in his fall. Her drama is portrayed with overpowering magnificence in Kleist's *Penthesilea*. In the image of Medusa and that of the Furies the ancient saga also reflects the horror inspired by the woman who has fallen. Even the belief in witches during Christian centuries, however tragically it may have erred in individual instances, signifies in its deeper implications the justification of the aversion against the woman who has become unfaithful to her metaphysical destiny. It is only the monstrous triviality exhibited today in the decline of woman that fails to arouse a similar horror. Obviously the story of the fall recurs continuously. In a deeper sense woman is the cause of every defection, not only because she is the mother within whose womb sinners are formed, but also because every fall, even the fall of man, is consummated within the sphere that has in a special sense been entrusted to woman.

As woman in rebellion stands at the beginning of human history so also she stands at the conclusion of all history. It is not the man who is the specifically apocalyptic expression of the human being; for the essential characteristic of the "latter days" is precisely that the form of the man disappears, since he is no longer capable of controlling the naked forces of destruction in manly fashion. For this reason also, St. John's Apocalypse does not present the antichrist as a human being, but as a beast rising out of the abyss. Woman, however, according to St. John, is recognizable as an apocalyptic figure. Only a woman who has become disloyal to her destiny can portray that absolute barrenness of the world which must inevitably cause its death and destruction.

If the sign of the woman is "Be it done unto me," which means the readiness to conceive or, when expressed in religious terms, the will to be blessed, then there is always distress when the woman no longer wills to conceive, no longer desires to be blessed. This does not apply only in a biological sense. To the ascending line which is the hierarchy of surrender corresponds a descending line of refusals, and a whole chasm yawns between the tragically heroic refusal of the amazon and the apocalyptic refusal of the woman. Just as the man under the sway of shameless powers which he should control loses his human dignity,

9

so the woman loses it as a whore, and it is the "great whore" of the Apocalypse which presents the image of the end of time.

The whore signifies the radical destruction of the *fiat* concept when surrender gives place to that last expression of inner refusal which is prostitution. The word does not mean a judgment pronounced against individuals from among the poorest of all women; for the whore herself represents her own judgment because she does not serve in the capacity of one who co-operates in the spirit of humility and love. She serves but as an object, and the object avenges itself through domination over the man who has fallen prey to dark forces. Thus she rises triumphantly, the enslaver of his passions. The whore as utter barrenness denotes the image of death. As mistress she stands for the rule of utter destruction.

The apocalypse of the latter days is preceded by the apocalypses of individual periods and cultural cycles. This means in regard to our own day that religious defection in unheard-of dimensions is becoming distinctly visible in the empiric manifestation of womanhood. The withdrawal of the veil, like the veil itself, is deeply symbolic. We have said that all the great expressions of woman's life show her as concealed. The bride, the widow, and the nun are the bearers of the same symbol. The outer gesture is never without significance; for, as it issues from a reality, so does it also represent that reality. From this point of view certain fashions become monstrous betrayals; in fact, they contribute to the dismantling of woman in the actual sense of the word. To unveil woman amounts to a destruction of her mystery.

The woman who does not surrender herself, even in the sphere of the senses, and is dedicated only to the most miserable of all cults, that of her own body, and this amid conditions of widespread distress among her fellow human beings, represents a degeneration that has torn asunder the very last of the bonds connecting her with her metaphysical destiny. When this happens it is no longer the innocently childlike face of feminine

10

vanity that is looking at us; in its stead, ghostly and banal, a countenance emerges that denotes the absolute opposite to the image of God, the faceless mask of femininity. This, rather than theoretical atheism, is the ghastly expression of contemporary godlessness. With this, our thought goes back to its beginning, to the revelation of the inviolate image of the divine, in the dogma of the Immaculate Conception.

The proclamation of a dogma is always the response to a specific religious emergency. The Marian dogma, as we have seen, when formulated in its most general terms means the co-operation of the creature in the Redemption of mankind. It is only from this definition that its tremendous meaning for our own age first dawns upon us. Divine grace never changes; it is the co-operation of the creature which in these days gives evidence of change to a growing extent.

In this connection it is of utmost importance that in recent years the longing of many nations for Mary has become so articulate. The apparitions of La Salette, Lourdes, and Fatima (to mention only the best known which also are the ones formally recognized by the Church) were the answer to this longing, and the recent proclamation of the conclusive Marian dogma, the one of the Assumption of the Blessed Mother into heaven, is but the significant result of these events. Even among Catholics this dogma has often been misunderstood. This is due not only to certain popular exaggerations of the veneration of Mary, but especially to the ephemerally rationalistic mode of thinking of modern man. We should not be surprised at this when even philosophy nowadays has become used to dispensing with its most precious jewel, which is metaphysics.

However, this youngest dogma now rises to a transcendental vision of the image of Mary, and in so doing puts the seal of approval upon a popular Catholic belief upheld through many centuries, a belief joyously expressed in the high feast of the Assumption. Great religious art had long anticipated Mary's assumption into heaven. Filippo Lippi's sublime painting in the church of Santa Maria sopra Minerva in Rome reflected the jubilant mood of her transfigured countenance. Fra Angelico let a golden crown rest on her head, while Dante Alighieri in his Divine Comedy praised not so much her appearance in earthly life as her blessedness hereafter to indicate that surrender in time leads to beatitude in heaven. We must realize that such beatitude refers not only to the Church as a whole, but to the individual soul and its physical body as well. The Virgin of Nazareth, of course, was the unique antecedent type of this transfiguration. In her it became a promise, and she could depend on Christ's word: "Father I will that where I am, they also whom thou has given me may be with me" (Jn. 17:24).

Let us now go back to the interpretation of Mary's significance here on earth. Precisely because of her co-operation, hers may well be the most powerful help to an endangered faith because she is the true conqueror of religious apostasy. This is what the Litany of Loreto means when it praises Mary as Queen of Angels, because as such she also is the queen of the fighter-angel, St. Michael. The litany also means this when it elevates Mary to the title of Queen of Apostles, for she is the one without whose aid even the apostolic message would not be effective. The very invocation, Queen of the Most Holy Rosary, has this same import, for prayer, too, does not become a real experience without the willingness and the readiness of the human heart to engage in it. The Marian dogma, then, implies not only the co-operation of the creature in Mary, but also that of the whole created universe.

Every religious emergency is but the well-house of a more universal distress. The profound connection between godlessness and judgment, namely, the obvious fact that a disturbance in the heart of life must upset all the realms of the outer life, has been lost sight of and is no longer a general conviction of our time. On the other hand, our present age has obtained the most imposing and at the same time awe-inspiring evidence of this truth that has ever been given to an era. The belief in Mary as the power conquering religious apostasy is therefore but a supreme expression of the faith in her as Mother of Perpetual Help.

Woman has, in the ultimate sense of the word, been the "bearer" of salvation. This does not apply to the sphere of religion alone; but because it is true in this sphere, it is also generally valid. The thought that peoples and nations, if they are to prosper, need good mothers, expresses, in addition to its obvious, biological truth, the even deeper truth that the world of the spirit also desires, not only the guidance of man, but likewise the motherly care of woman. At this point the two lines intersect. If on the one hand the creature refuses to co-operate with the Redemption, it has on the other hand usurped Redemption. Faith in self-redemption as man's belief in his own creative powers is the specifically masculine delusion of our secularized age and is at the same time the explanation of all its failures. Nowhere is the creature a redeemer on its own, but it should co-operate in the work of redemption. Creative power can only be received, and man is no exception, for he, too, must conceive the creative spirit in the sign of Mary, in humility and surrender, or he will not receive it at all. In its stead, again and again he will accept only the spirit, to use Goethe's words, "that he comprehends," a spirit which in the final analysis can comprehend nothing; for the world may indeed be moved by the strength of the man, but it will be blessed, in the true sense of the word, only in the sign of the woman.

Surrender to God is the only absolute power that the creature possesses. Only the handmaid of the Lord is the Queen of Heaven. Wherever the creature co-operates with utmost sincerity, there the Mother of the Creator will appear, the Mother of Good Counsel. Wherever the creature becomes detached from self, the Mother Most Amiable, the Mother of Fair Love, comes to the aid of a tortured world. Wherever the nations of the earth are of good will, the Queen of Peace intercedes for them.

The redemption of man's world, however, is but an image of

the redemption from beyond. Again nature supplies the prelude as it were for the supernatural, and this prelude echoes through all the spheres of being. The bridal earth that opens to the seed also receives all that is mortal for its last repose. As all life rises out of surrender, so also in surrender it ends. But the earth which receives the dead is not itself eternity; it only returns the dying to eternity, and the dying creature itself becomes the seed of a resurrection. Mary is the patroness of the dying, the Mother of Mercy. Hers is a dual aspect, for the patroness of the dying individual is also the patroness of the dying earth, the earth that at some time will disintegrate. This means that Mary is at the same time the Madonna of the Apocalypse.

The great Spanish painter El Greco has represented the Madonna of the Apocalypse under the perspective of the Immaculate Conception. The strangely frightening and ill-boding loveliness of the landscape that he places at her feet reflects the atmosphere of the fallen world before the appearance of Christ, and is at the same time prophetic of the mood of destruction that will precede His second coming. It expresses that groan and travail of the creature which, according to the words of St. Paul, is still in the pangs of birth. Apocalypse is not only a descent; it is also a dawning, and the returning Christ comes as the Judge of the world in the strength of the Creator of the world. The Marian dogma is not given its ultimate confirmation until we reach the gates of the world to come. The patroness of the dying, the Madonna of the Apocalypse as the Immaculate Conception, means the promise of a new heaven and a new earth.

So the motif of the Morning Star appears again, the star that heralds the sun yet pales in its presence. Just as the Litany of Loreto, suddenly interrupting its powerful invocations to Mary, casts itself as it were at the feet of the Lamb of God, so the Eternal Feminine kneels in the presence of Eternal Divinity when it has that noble power to attract of which Goethe speaks. The ultimate mystery of the Immaculata is the Creator. The

14

ultimate mystery of the Co-Redemptrix is the Redeemer. And the glory of the Holy Spirit, of Uncreated Love itself, is the crown, but also the veil, the last, the everlasting veil upon the head of the Virgin Mother.

THE WOMAN IN TIME

Woman in time! This apparently would signify fully half of all human existence and activity and therefore the half of history. It is evident, however, that not woman but man and his work make up historical life. Not only does man dominate the political activities of nations, but he also determines the rise and decline of their culture. Furthermore, and this is perhaps the most significant: even religious life, which, as we have seen, is in special measure entrusted to woman, has in its large historical manifestations been fashioned by man, and he primarily is its representative.

Whenever one listens for the voice of the centuries, it is man's voice that one hears; while woman, with certain exceptions, appears but as the timeless abundance of a living silence which accompanies or carries his voice. Does this mean that the surrendering power of the Cosmos, which is the mystery of woman, implies a further surrender, in the sense of a metaphysical renunciation in regard to life historically determined? Does the religious element mean renunciation of power? Shall one say that its kingdom is not of this world? Or do both questions imply that one must reach down to a more profound level? Do they stress a new standard of historical evaluation? Clearly this problem must be posed within a more comprehensive framework, and woman in time becomes a question of the woman of our time.

It is known that in our days the standards of historical evaluation have undergone a transformation. Those of the last epoch were derived largely from the high esteem with which it regarded personality. The general public found its dignity and its value represented in the great individual personality. The present time, on the contrary, presses beyond the merely personal element. It does not deny the significance of the great personality; but it no longer finds an ultimate value in its predominance. The importance of even the greatest individual now lies in his surrender to the general welfare, and in the measure of his contribution in this respect is his value determined. Hence the new standard of historical evaluation is no longer personality, but surrender. From this different perspective the significance of the sexes in the course of history must be examined anew, that is, according to the dominating forces that are their fundamental endowment.

If one inquires into the original laws of life, biological research confirms the assertion that woman does not in herself either represent or exercise the great, historically effective talents, but she is nevertheless their silent carrier. If one seeks the source of outstanding personal qualifications one must proceed from sons, not to their fathers, but to their mothers. To this fact a great number of highly gifted men and their mothers bear testimony. On the other hand, extraordinary men frequently have insignificant sons. This seems to indicate that man spends his strength in his own performance, while woman does not spend but transmits it. Man spends and exhausts himself in his work and in giving his talent gives himself with it, while woman gives even the talent away to the coming generation. Her endowment then, appears as equal to that of the man; but it is not for the woman herself, it is for the generation. With this fact, the dominant trend of the present day comes to the surface. Woman's innate endowment is not defined by her personality which it transcends, and because of this she is properly aligned with the very trend that constitutes the standard of value of this present age.

Seen in this light it is also of symbolic significance that the woman on an average lives longer than the man. The latter represents the historical situation of his time, while the woman stands for the generation. Man signifies the eternal value of the moment; woman, the unending sequence of the generations. Man is the rock upon which the times rest; woman is the stream that bears them onward. The rock is formed, the stream is fluid; individual personality belongs primarily to the man, while universality is the characteristic of the woman. The personal is the unique and therefore the transient; it consumes its capital, but the universal conserves it.

Like the individual woman who in general lives longer than the individual man, so also the female line of generation survives that of the male. When we say of families and races that they have died out, we refer as a rule only to the male branch; the female line frequently continues for longer periods and perhaps never becomes extinct. We rarely realize that the blood of the great families of the past, as for instance the Hohenstaufens or even the Carolingians, may be traced down to the present day through the daughter families in which the name of the male branch has disappeared.

As woman primarily denotes not personality but its surrender, so also the endurance that she is able to give to her descendants is not self-assertion, but something purchased at the expense of submerging herself into the universal stream of succeeding generations. It is at this point that we encounter the second basic motif of woman, that of the veil. Even the experience which is most fundamentally her own, the passing on of life and heritage of blood, remains nameless and concealed as far as she herself is concerned. The great stream of all the forces that have made and will continue to make history proceeds through the woman who bears no other name than that of mother. Our time does justice to this elemental fact when it values woman first of all as mother.

Beside the mother stands the single woman. That the majority of women who cannot become mothers today belong to the generation that has suffered from war is also symbolic. Their hope of fulfillment in marriage, and with it that of man's protection and support, lies buried in the graves of Europe and Asia. The war of course only brings out more strongly what has always and everywhere been true. So far as the mother is concerned, woman's problem is relatively easy to solve. Nature has already provided the solution. However, all problems of economic need are beyond the range both of nature and of metaphysical reality with which we are here concerned. The inner weight of the question does not bear upon the mother, but upon the unmarried woman.

That our time avoids coming to terms with her is understandable. It entertains the naïve conviction that the significance of the unmarried woman comes to the fore in the bride. From a positive standpoint this age sees her only in girlish expectancy; negatively, the disappointed old maid, or, what is worse, the contented bachelor girl, would appear to be the counterpart. Consequently our period sees the unmarried woman only as a condition or as something tragic. A mere condition passes away; a tragedy may perhaps be averted in the future. The question here, however, concerns not only a condition, but a value that is retained even in case of tragedy. The one whom we negatively call the unmarried woman is in a positive sense the virgin. Obviously, she is not the only aspect of the unmarried woman, but she is her most natural expression.

In other times a virgin held a definite position of dignity. Not only does Christianity approve of her, but many of the values that it emphasizes have been anticipated also in pre-Christian times. Names of mountains and of constellations proclaim the virgin; while her character as expressed in a Diana or a Minerva, though differently conceived and motivated, is in a natural sense no less impressive than that of the Christian saint. The exalted honor that the Germanic woman of old enjoyed was linked with the appreciation of virginity. To this the terrible, punitive laws of the ancient Saxons bear testimony, when they direct themselves with equal severity against the assault upon the chastity of a virgin and against the woman who had fallen.

Like the priestess of Vesta, the Germanic prophetess also was a virgin. Both the German saga and the German fairy tale, despite their pagan sources, show us time and again the meaning of the virgin who is pure. In the German saga she possesses even a redemptive power, and up to the later Middle Ages the irreproachable virgin could obtain pardon for a man condemned to death.

She alone could avert an inevitable curse and break a spell of magic that could not otherwise be overcome. To borrow Theodore Haecker's[1] beautiful expression, which he applied to the classical ages, the pagan period of early Germanic history, in its belief in the saving power of a virgin, became "like an advent" preparing the way for the Christian faith in Mary.

The Litany of Loreto calls Mary the Virgin of Virgins and the Queen of Virgins. The Mother of all mothers remains, as mother, the virgin undefiled. By the dogma of the perpetual virginity of the Mother of God, the Church expresses not only the inviolable purity of Mary, but establishes for all time the meaning of virginity in itself, placing its dignity beside the dignity of motherhood.

This concept of virginity which the dogma has worked out has come to life in the Christian era of great occidental art, illuminating at the same time both the pre-Christian and the post-Christian epochs. Whenever art that was truly great represented the virgin, it did not express a temporary condition such as maidenly expectation, nor did it depict a hope destroyed; but it heralded a mystery. In the magnificent sculptures of antiquity as well as during the golden age of Christian plastic and pictorial art, virginity in its most authentic expression appears in an absolute sense. It is not the outward loveliness, its aspect of inviolability, but the inner character that is its secret.

This quality is apparent in classical poetry even more, if possible, than in great visual art. It is striking to observe how fre-

---

[1] An outstanding German Catholic poet and writer who died in Munich shortly after World War II.

quently poetry exalts woman in her virginal type rather than in that of wife and mother. Antigone and Beatrice, Iphigenia and Tasso's Princess are virginal figures and can be properly understood only as such. Schiller in his presentation of Joan of Arc did not grasp the idea of the saint; but the concept of virginity he recognized as undestructible, for the power of her personality was rooted in it. At this point the life lines of the virgin and the man intersect, for the man also values virginity as aiding and adding intensity to the pursuit of his highest achievement. This is the meaning of the well-known concept that priests, soldiers, and political leaders, in fact all whose duty it is to devote their lives fully to a certain cause, should remain unmarried.

Thus from dogma, history, saga, and art, the idea of virginity emerges, not as a transitory condition or a tragedy, but as a value and a power. To recognize this means for our day to face a double difficulty. God no longer stands at the center of our thinking as He did in that of an earlier day. Instead, man has moved into the foreground, not as an individual, but as a link in the chain of generations. The virgin, however, has her place, not within the generation, but at its conclusion. She no longer holds her position on the progressively advancing line of an earthly infiniteness, but she is identified with that single moment of her personal life which seems so limited in time. From this position she exacts faith in the ultimate value of the individual as such, a value not justified by mere human qualities. In other words her formal meaning is the religious exaltation and affirmation of a person's value, as directly and ultimately related to God alone.

Like the solitary flower of the mountains, far up at the fringe of eternal snows, that has never been looked upon by the eye of man; like the far distant beauty of the polar zones and the deserts of the earth, that are not easily accessible to the services and purposes of man, the virgin proclaims that the creature has significance, but only as a glow from the eternal radiance of the Creator. The virgin stands at the margin of the mysteries of all that is seemingly wasted and unfulfilled. Like those who have died in early youth and have not lived to unfold their most glorious gifts, she stands at the brink of all that appears to have failed. Her inviolability, which, if it be purity, always includes a depth of pain, denotes the sacrifice that is the price for an insight into the infinite value of a person. This explains why the liturgy always places the virgin beside the martyr who, like her, bears witness to the absolute value of the soul in the holocaust of his (or her) earthly life.

From the religious significance of the virgin it becomes obvious and imperative that orders of women demand the vow of virginity. In this connection it becomes equally evident that everything temporal derives its real meaning from that which is eternal. Manifestly, wherever it becomes necessary to reach down to the deepest roots of a matter, it is the Catholic dogma that has worked out the essential underlying thought. At this point perhaps we should glance briefly at the religious ceremony for the consecration of virgins. The words of the Preface preceding it are decisive: "While respecting the nuptial blessing resting upon the sacred state of marriage, there should still be noble souls who, spurning the physical union entered into by man and wife, strive after the mystery it signifies and devote their entire love to the mystery suggested by marriage,"[2] that is, the mystery of charity.

The mystery of love, therefore, hovers over both the nuptial Mass and the dedication of virgins; for the consecrated virgin is the spouse of Christ. Agreeing in this respect with the world, the Church also affirms that the virgin is as one destined to be a bride; but she does not see her only as the partner of a man. For one charged moment the profound association between the Marian dogma and all the mysteries of womanhood becomes strikingly clear. Mary's perpetual virginity signifies the espousal and the overshadowing of the Holy Spirit. At the consecration

---

[2] Ancient bridal prayer of the *Sacramentarium Fuldense*.

of a virgin this means the acceptance of her *Fiat mihi*, her "Be it done unto me," in regard to the unmarried state. On the part of God it is the fulfillment of the virgin's life through the mystery of a charity resting upon a higher than natural plane. The value of the person as such, which must be recognized in every human being, can be established only when such value exists before God, and it is actually established in the religious mystery of charity. From this assurance a shaft of light descends straight through all the levels of solitary feminine existence. In the language of dogma this means the appearance of the vicarious element as a concept.

Representation in its religious meaning, translated into secular language, is the co-operating responsibility of all for all. This, in the light of the concept of the Mystical Body of Christ, expresses the religious pinnacle of a thought which our age has undertaken to proclaim far and wide over the secular field, by demanding the conquest of individualism. It is only the lack of true insight into the essence of the dogma, which still is so tenacious a remnant of a liberal tradition, that bars our generation from understanding how much it depends on Christian truth. Just as the work of a creative genius does not belong only to him who fashioned it, so also perfection and the loving deed do not belong only to the perfect one or the loving one; they are the property of all. Only to a time blinded by subjectivism could it seem impossible that the merits of the saints are of benefit to their brethren upon earth. Applied to our theme, this is to say that the mystery of charity inherent in the consecration of virgins spreads out, as it were, upon the whole world. The Spouse of Christ helps to explain the hidden meaning that belongs to every virgin, a meaning which even the least and most inconspicuous among them unconsciously defends.

It is here among the least and most inconspicuous that the concept of the virgin peculiar to our time, inasmuch as its tragic aspects are at stake, fits into our picture. The involuntary sacrifice stands in contrast to the voluntary one; the mystery of iniquity to the mystery of charity; instead of the "be it done unto me" we have the "no" of the creature. For the woman who does not recognize in her virginity a value that has its relationship to God, the unmarried state and childlessness are really a profound tragedy. Both to marriage and to children, woman is spiritually and physically more intimately disposed than man, and to be deprived of them can lead her to regard her own existence as utterly futile. However, the deeper meaning of her unmarried state and her childlessness remains unimpaired by this apparent uselessness. In fact, by an extreme penetration of this problem we may grasp its intense significance exactly at this point. For it is perhaps only an existence seemingly the most worthless that can most fully establish the ultimate sense of the value of a person as such. In every other instance there would be danger lest some achievement, and not the personality itself, constitute its intrinsic worth.

At this point religious dialectics crosses worldly reasoning. The contemplative life, which from a religious angle stresses man's final destiny in God, from a natural perspective means for the most part a lack of achievement in the world. In a similar way the feeble voice of the solitary woman, whose life in the world has remained unfulfilled, echoes in sisterly fashion the avowal of surrender on the part of the Spouse of Christ, because the transcendental ultimate meaning of the person only comes to the fore when there is no visible accomplishment on its part. In our own day we face this very problem when the question is raised regarding the meaning and value of the person and whether it still has a meaning at all.

It would be a mistake, if in this connection we were to think first of the individual personality, for the individual personality is of a singular albeit temporal value only. Christian Redemption is concerned not with the personality, but with the human person as a whole, its end being ordained for God. The person is an eternal value, and history gains its meaning and purpose only through such a value. Without eternal values there would be historical sequences, but no history. Against such a background we understand the dual significance of woman in history. While motherhood passes on the history-making capabilities of the man to its own generation, virginity has the function of safeguarding the human person as such which is the prerequisite of man's ability to bring about achievements of historical significance.

Once we acknowledge the religious import of the virgin, we easily understand her temporal significance. The virgin who sacrifices marriage and motherhood in order to represent the worth of the solitary person secures by this very renunciation both marriage and motherhood. Just as she herself would not remain a virgin if she did not respect the concept of marriage for her own person, so she defends thereby the married state of her sister women. For the majority of the latter the dissolution of the marriage tie becomes inevitable as soon as the unmarried woman loses her respect for virginity. Without the virgin there is no married state, and therefore no really protected motherhood. She who concludes the generation to render the final worth of the individual person secure, likewise guards the safety of the generation, and she does it by very reason of her respect for the value of a person.

As both wedlock and virginity are anchored in the mystery of charity, so are they anchored in the human person whose value is the foundation of marriage. Hence the ultimate worth of the person does not devolve only upon the person, but also upon the generation. If these relationships are practically unknown to human society, this again but signifies the veil which conceals all womanly living. Without the veil these relationships obviously would lack their final authenticity and hence their most profound power; for decisive results have their origin in hidden sources.

This brings us face to face with the concept of the virgin as a power. The man also, as we have noted, is aware of the

25

meaning of virginity in his own life, as an intensifying force toward the highest achievement. Every conservation of strength at one point implies the possibility of higher potentials at another. In this sense virginity is not an exclusion of efficiency, but rather an accentuation of it — in a different way. With reference to woman this means that her capacity for love which finds no outlet in a family of her own is automatically extended to the great human family as a whole.

When the unmarried woman cannot realize her potentiality for physical motherhood and so diverts her energy to a practical purpose, her impulse is one of giving as it exists both biologically and psychologically in the mother. Clearly the concept of virginity is related to the one of spiritual motherhood, but this we shall discuss later. We are dealing at the moment with woman in time. The mother, however, and also the spiritual mother, is not bound by time; she is timeless. Therefore our concern right now is not the achievement of woman as a mother metaphorically, but with her actual achievement in the realm of the spirit.

Virginity, then, denotes in a special manner a capacity, a release for action. In this light we understand why the drama which is built entirely upon action so definitely prefers the virginal figure of woman to that of the wife and mother. The same law applies both to the creative writer and to the figure he creates. Consequently not only Antigone and Iphigenia, but also the mystic Hroswitha of Gandersheim and the poetess Annette von Droste-Hülshoff, are essentially virginal.

Thus the woman whose strength is not limited to her own generation, rightly and naturally feels the urge to make her contribution toward the historical and cultural life of her people. The more so is this justified since the form of such co-operation on her part is largely determined by the fact that woman always comes to the rescue when there is need. Her historical and cultural activity repeats, as it were, in the field of objective achievement that which holds good within the scope of a generation; when the male line fails, the daughter substitutes for the right of succession. The need of woman coming to the rescue indicates that too many other demands are being made of man, or that there is some lack of man power. The home front of women in times of war has shown this impressively.

The independent advance of woman into the cultural field is, therefore, always significant. When this happens the face of the Eternal Woman becomes visible for a moment, above the woman in time; for woman coming to the rescue means that her activity, strictly speaking, is not activity in itself, but surrender, which is but another form of the womanly "Be it done unto me." Accordingly, woman withdraws of her own accord, when the need for her activity no longer exists. In this circumstance woman's objective achievement finds its extraordinary, if largely unappreciated and therefore deeply veiled recognition; but it finds there also its limitations. For the significance of woman in historical and cultural life cannot ultimately depend upon her factual and practical co-operation; its roots are much more profound.

Just as the virgin as such stands at the border of the mystery enshrouding all that seems wasted and unfulfilled in life, so she stands at the borderline of these same mysteries as a person capable of achievement. The veil motif recurs with the fact that, in the order of achievement, woman's contribution at best can occupy but a secondary place, since it but seldom penetrates the full depth and power of the feminine soul and but rarely makes it possible for her to assert her specifically feminine influence in the cultural field. Ordinarily she adjusts herself to masculine standards and by this very adjustment is outdistanced by man's original achievement. The veil motif is still discernible, however, when woman actually does attain to some ultimate height of achievement, for then a charismatic vocation becomes more evident in her work than in the work of a man. The charismatic character of a talent or an activity signifies, as we know, not only its extraordinary, but primarily its religious quality. It is therefore not an accident when genius that is essentially feminine becomes manifest only in the religious sphere. Few women of the secular world can measure up to the greatness of a Hildegard von Bingen, a Joan of Orleans, a Catherine of Siena. It is understandable, therefore, that the very Church which has man as the exclusive carrier of her hierarchy should acknowledge the specifically feminine charismatic endowment.

Once again we need religious standards of interpretation. The concept *Spouse of Christ* has clarified the meaning of virginity. In the same way the specific achievement of feminine genius becomes understandable by means of the charismatic idea. God alone can lift the veil under which He Himself has hidden woman, and even such a lifting of the veil would only mean an even more profound concealment. Charism does not mean the power of producing one's own achievement; it means, on the contrary, to obliterate oneself to the point of becoming an instrument of God.

While previously we considered the value of the person as apart from any achievement, now by the charismatic vocation we are implying an achievement as distinct from the person who accomplishes it. Charism itself becomes a veil. To woman's natural ability of leaping into a breach corresponds, on a loftier level, her being called to shoulder specific responsibilities, especially in crucial emergencies,. The highest vocation of woman is always a last expedient, and we grasp the astonishing significance of a St. Catherine or a St. Joan only when we know who had already failed on the missions that later became theirs.

By the same token by which an existence, worthless according to the standard of achievement, illustrates the ultimate value of the person, so the essential characteristic of a vocation is demonstrated where apparently there is no vocation. This sheds light upon the reason why the greatest figures in the history of humanity were precisely those who at the beginning of their careers seemed insignificant or unfit in the eyes of their contemporaries, and why their importance revealed itself late or despite all contrary expectations. As the humanly valuable is always in danger, at the final issue, of becoming evident in some achievement, rather than in the worth of the person who accomplished it, so in the matter of a supreme vocation there is equal danger lest the emphasis be not upon the vocation, but upon the degree of endowment possessed by the person that is called. This would mean that the latter were promoting not only the calling but the person itself.

In every great achievement there is always, however, an added quality that surpasses not only the capabilities but even the original intentions of the person responsible for it. In other words, it is the splendor of the divine creative will shining through the human achievement that constitutes its actual worth. To prove this the person who seemingly has no vocation must sometimes be the very one who is chosen. The invisible pillar of that which has come to pass must become visible. This is the symbolic meaning of the charismatic woman. The basic reason that she had been chosen in preference to the man, lies in the fact that by nature her personality is more easily able to efface itself into becoming a mere instrument or vessel. To bear the charism means to be the handmaid of the Lord.

Thus even woman's most amazing achievement, which is charismatic, remains entirely within the boundaries of the feminine, along the line of mere co-operation, along the path of Mary. Precisely because of this she uplifts the lesser achievement of her unassuming sister-woman. Upon her she sheds the ray of light fallen upon herself from the resplendent mystery of the Eternal Woman. The concept of the vicarious power appears once more: the sisterly colloquy continues between the Spouse of Christ and the woman in the world who seems to have missed her calling.

The quality of mere co-operation that is evident also in the charismatic woman serves to throw some light on the mystery of why feminine achievement that is not charismatic inevitably occupies a second or third place. The reason does not hinge upon the question of whether or not a woman is more or less gifted; it lies in the nature and in the task of woman. That which we have said about the value of the person is valid also in this instance. A final tapering of the thought discloses the inconspicuous achievement as constituting the actual mystery of woman, her meaning not as a visible but an invisible pillar of historical life.

As the virgin represents the inherent value of the person independently of every achievement, so woman as here considered demonstrates the final value of every gift and every achievement, entirely independent of success or recognition. She expresses the reality, the total impact of the unknown, the seemingly ineffectual, the hidden, as it is in God. She represents, as do the lone graves of a lost war, the final import of all history. Above and beyond the visible world, she answers for the invisible.

*   *   *

The concept of co-operation to which we have just referred opens a further vista. While the teaching of the Church concerning the virgin brings to life the concept of the Spouse of Christ, it helps us understand at the same time the concept of the spouse of man. The same mystery that hovers over the consecration of a virgin broods also, as we have seen, over the nuptial Mass. "O Lord our God," we read in an old marriage prayer, "You have willed that for the continuance of the human race one generation should be created from another through the mystery of charity." This mystery of charity, here interpreted as a mystery of creation, in secular language indicates the creative significance of the polarity between masculine and feminine forces. Upon the principle of their co-operation all life depends, and the extent of their power ranges over the whole universe, even over the domain of intellectual and cultural accomplishment.

It is, then, no longer a question of the independent cultural achievement of woman, but it is now her role in co-operation with man, her place within this work which concerns us. It is now the acceptance of a mystery of charity we are concerned with, also with regard to cultural and spiritual pursuits, and this amounts to the recognition of the nuptial character of culture. However, at this juncture an apparent difficulty arises. If we apply the strict analogy with the natural mystery of creation, a woman's part should be spiritual conception and birth. She would then play the role of a mother in regard to the work of man. But the mystery of charity, as a nuptial mystery, is not yet that of the mother, but of the bride, and the bride stands between the virgin and the mother.

These two concepts which merge in Mary's title as the Eternal Woman, in the magnificent landscape which surrounds woman in dogmatic theology, in a sense constitute the twin summits, or basic pillars. Between them stretches out a wide, often fertile valley, the great kingdom which belongs to woman as the companion to man. What is at stake is an independent domain, and as we view it we must realize the importance of establishing clearly that every one of these three timelessly valid aspects of woman's life — virgin, bride, and mother — denote the fulfillment of woman's life in its entirety, but each within its own proper scope. The association between these various forms, their merging one into the other, does not indicate a contingency by which one would depend on the other so that perhaps the essentially womanly role would pertain only to the mother. The bride is, to be sure, the first step to the mother; but she is likewise the bearer of an independent feminine mystery.

The Church conveys this meaning by accepting childless marriage as entirely valid and indissoluble. This indicates that the bride as standing between the virgin and the mother is not only the future bearer of the generation, but as bride she is primarily a person in her own right. The sacramental character of marriage does not only consecrate the generation, but it also unites a person to a person. It is consequently not solely a matter of the propagation of the race, but also of the salvific import in the mutual love of two human beings, of their spiritual responsibility one for the other on their way to God.

Therefore the mystery of charity in the nuptial Mass intimates not only the corporal, but also the spiritual fertility of marriage. According to the interpretation of the Church, man and wife are not only of one flesh, but also of one spirit. The bride who in one aspect of her being represents the future mother retains on the other hand, not in a natural but in a spiritual sense, the virginal character. She retains it as bride.

It is the bride who signifies the essential mystery of the spouse and as she is an independent mystery so is she also a permanent one. Popular custom does not err in still seeing a bride in the wife of the silver wedding. Although she be a mother, the woman, in so far as she responds to man's love for her, retains her bridal character. To see in the bride nothing more than the maiden of the wedding day is to give the mystery a purely naturalistic interpretation. In her response to the man who loves her, the wife remains a bride all her life long. In similar fashion the wedding day repeats itself as long as her life lasts, and the bridal quality of the woman corresponds to love in its unending regeneration.

Some of the radiance inherent in the aspect of the Virgin Spouse which we find expressed in the term Bride of Christ also is reflected upon the spouse of a man. At the same time, out of the concept of eternal bridals, the aspect of Mary the Eternal Woman rises upon her, for Mary whose title alone unites the Virgin and the Mother, is the Bride of the Holy Spirit. Mary, however, is also the one who, on Pentecost morning in the company of the Apostles, receives the Holy Spirit. Scripture calls the Holy Spirit both the Spirit of Love and the Creator Spirit, and from this dual designation the twofold character of the mystery of charity becomes evident.

Here, as everywhere, we see that the Church has developed the decisive aspects. As the spouse of Christ throws a conclusive

32

light upon the problem of virginity, so the wife, sacramentally bound, constitutes the culminating point of the spousal concept. Behind her, the fullness of creative potentialities which exist between man and woman extends in its spiritual lines to the romance not sacramentally bound, to the woman friend of a man, to his mistress, to the associate of his work. Upon all of them falls the illumination of the bridal Mass. To the salvific, creative significance that two people have for one another in the context of this sacramental reality, corresponds in the secular sphere a creative companionship, the unique spiritual meaning of two people for one another. There is also a mystery of charity that belongs to the natural realm, as a mystery of spiritual creation between a man and a woman; there is also a spouse who is the bride of man's spirit.

Since we are dealing with the cultural sphere, we must remember at this point the celebrated companionships which exemplify this thought vividly. Dante and Beatrice, Michelangelo and Vittoria Colonna, Hoelderlin and Diotima, Goethe and Frau von Stein, Richard Wagner and Mathilde Wesendonk — to mention just these few great ones — point the way.

> Through my eyes you entered into me
> And forced me thus, to grow to mighty stature —

Thus Michelangelo wrote in one of his sonnets to Vittoria Colonna. Hoelderlin expresses this same thought even more clearly to Diotima:

> Marveling I look upon you; I hear voices and sweet song
> As from an ancient time, and the music of strings;
> Brightly now my spirit wings
> Spheres.

As the individual expands into the we, dual creativeness becomes evident, the forces of spiritual creation emerge with lively impact to manifest the bridal character of culture.

Woman's part in this spiritual mystery of charity is the same as it is throughout historical and cultural life. Only in rare cases does this co-operation become fruitful for the woman in a creation of her own, as for example Elizabeth Barrett Browning's *Sonnets from the Portuguese* or Marianne Weber's[3] splendid description of the life and work of her husband. Woman for the most part vanishes into the creative work of man or becomes visible only in the homage offered by it to her. Of the complete disappearance of even a highly gifted woman into a man's life-work, Marianne von Willemer[4] is an outstanding example; for we know that her participation in Goethe's *Westoestlicher Divan* was greater than we can accurately determine. Fundamentally, however, there is no need to define such an active part played by a woman, for the very fact that woman does not as a rule co-operate actively the better expresses the essential character of her feminine participation.

The concept of the spouse as the bride of the masculine spirit means that the spouse as the other part of man constitutes the other half of Being as a whole. The beautiful expression found in the Bible that the man must "know" the woman applies also to spiritual creation. In her he "knows" the other dimension of human existence. Polarity is totality and is the prerequisite of every truly great work. Only from this angle does Hoelderlin's almost overwhelming avowal to Diotima become understandable:

> When in me God's inspiration
> Dawns for me upon her brow.

Actually it is not God who dawns; the whole of divine creation dawns, the other half of existence without which even God cannot inspire a supremely great work. This is the exalted meaning in Dante's journey from hell to heaven when at the outset the man, Virgil, leads him, but later Beatrice, the beloved of his youth, becomes his guide. One cannot say of this other dimension that it actually manifests itself, but rather that it

---

[3] Outstanding German sociologist.
[4] Friend of Goethe.

gives itself. The man "knows" the woman, but the woman is "known" by her attitude of surrender.

On the spiritual plane with which we are concerned, it is not a question of woman taking up a man's thoughts, nor of a spiritual co-operation and joint elaboration of such thoughts. This may happen now and then, but it is only one form of the mystery of charity and not its essence. Neither does it mean merely an understanding accord on the part of the woman; this would be like a musical accompaniment. But here surrender is revelation; it is a gift. The woman, having surrendered herself to the man, under whatever form, brings to him the dowry of half a world.

In the surrender of the woman as a revelation of this other half of all creation consists her participation in man's spiritual and cultural achievements. Surrender is revelation, but a hidden one. Even in the other world Beatrice is at first veiled as she approaches Dante.

The revelation of the woman is so deeply concealed that there are times when the man utterly fails to recognize it as such. He believes to be envisioning less the woman than his own image.

> Then I know that I exist —

Hoelderlin says of Diotima's nearness to him. It is only in becoming aware of the other person's image that one's own is capable of assuming a specific form. Each has its rightful position only within the whole of creation, and only in the light of woman's nature does man's being also become evident. Totality does not mean the revelation only of the other half of being; it means the disclosure also of one's own half. As the woman may only be "known" by the man when he approaches her with profound love, so it is only in her love that he fully knows himself. This is the significance of the term *mirror* which so often appears in the testimony great writers give of their relationship to woman. Dante looks into this mirror when, on the

35

Mountain of Purgatory, Beatrice asks for his profession of faith. Under this perspective we understand the passionate desire with which a man has often struggled for a woman, and for her spiritual nearness; it is her spirituality that implies the prodigious dowry he can share through her alone.

The bride, as she stands between the virgin and the mother, stands also between person and generation, advancing a step, however, beyond the boundaries of the person. If the virgin has made secure for man that final and solitary value of culture which is the person, so likewise the bride assures him of the co-operation of half a world. As she rescues his life from its loneliness she also draws him spiritually beyond the limits of his own person. It is the presence of the womanly element which reveals the anonymous aspect of every great creative work.

We see, then, how under these perspectives the qualities essential to all that is womanly come to the surface, that is, woman's disposition to co-operate, and that of the veil. To express it in another way: in the anonymous element that is present in culture we recognize the invisible pillar or support of human history. Woman is not the operative but the co-operative influence; the co-operative, however, is also the co-creative. This line of thought obviously hinges on a specific understanding of the nature of all spiritual and intellectual activity.

With apparent justification one might raise the objection that there is no difference between the object of a creation and the subject of the author; and that, therefore, the mere inclusion of woman in the work of man does not as yet mean their being jointly engaged in a given undertaking. This, however, is an argument that applied only in the past age which was dominated by great personalities. Today we do not consider a great cultural achievement as the work of its originator only, but the very characteristic of such an achievement is the confluence of many participating streams contributing toward it. Our epoch expresses this awareness by the importance it attaches to the landscape and to the soil from which a spiritual work is drawn.

The creative personality is the spokesman for a chorus that is mute. Not only does he create, but through him something is being created. The true poet knows that his object shares with him in the act of creation. He is aware of its mysterious penetration into him, of its inspirations to him, often bordering upon the miraculous. Not only does a poet love his material; it is as though his material loved him. This explains Dante's words:

> . . . not always is the artist's striving meet
> To mould the work to fit his spirit's vision,
> For substance can be deaf, unable to respond.

The vanity or jealousy of a creative personality, therefore, always betrays a person who is not creative in the deep sense of the word. The truly creative person would refuse to be honored as the sole author of his work. To him it is obvious that its greatness and scope depend upon the participation of numerous elements.

This also helps us to understand the homage, often rapturous, that great poets have paid to woman. It is a jubilant tribute motivated by the knowledge of not working alone, for every profoundly and genuinely womanly personality, while inspiring the work of man, professes deep down the mystery of charity.

The creative process in which the individual genius and the woman who co-operates with him share, repeats itself in all the social aspects of cultural life. In this respect the history of Catholic religious orders as bearers of culture — and with culture we are here concerned — is enlightening. As the spiritual mystery of charity hovers over the great religious friendships of a St. Francis of Assisi and a St. Clare, a St. John of the Cross and a St. Teresa of Avila, a St. Francis de Sales and a St. Jane Frances de Chantal, so it rests upon the foundations associated with these names. The essence of the mystery is not only love, but also charity. Every great religious order of men as an instrument of culture has sought and found an order of women as its counterpart. The Opus Dei of the Benedictines, which signifies the praise of God as the indispensable prerequisite and innermost meaning of all culture, could never have realized its purpose of vicarious adoration on behalf of all creation if the woman's voice had been missing in its choir. The Order of St. Francis, which by a new spirit of love and poverty counteracted a cul· ture smothered with luxury, by its very ideals was tending toward renunciation and the willingness to surrender typical of woman. The asceticism and mysticism of St. Dominic find their supreme fulfillment, not only in the intellectual edifice of St. Thomas Aquinas or in Master Eckhart's depth of soul, but also in the practical activity of St. Catherine of Siena.

And Carmel, which in the light of our reasoning in this context denotes pre-eminently that inner freedom which assigns culture to its proper place by obviating from it the danger of becoming an idol, depends from its very beginning, by its intimate relation to Mary, on the participation of woman. Even the Society of Jesus which did not seek a feminine complement was forced to find it against its own intentions inasmuch as it became the vehicle of the last expression of culture that had a wide western scope, the baroque. However, St. Ignatius foresaw that a counterpart in a grouping of women could never succeed perfectly. The religious foundations of women built upon the Jesuit ideal of education show only some of its traits. It is the individual Christian woman in the world, not connected with a religious community, who comes nearest to the heroic impulse fundamental to this order which is not protected by monastic enclosure; nearest also to the unqualified dedication of the individual members to their widely divergent duties. As Carmel demonstrates the capacity for silent suffering that is in woman, so the solitary woman stands quietly in the midst of the world, heroically upholding the ramparts of Christianity. Thus the Society of Jesus, remote as it is from the ideal of the cloistered family, remains inspired by the spiritual mystery of charity.

This mystery of charity also inspires the manifold entirely secular associations in which men and women work together. Since they consist of both men and women, they never represent a mere co-operation, but also and always a relevancy to the totality of being. Even this last kind of association is related to the mystery of charity, if only as the last link.

Every sort of co-operation, even the most insignificant, between man and woman is, in its bearing upon the wholeness of life, of far greater import than associations that are purely masculine or purely feminine. Naturally, such associations have their definite purposes inasmuch as they are dedicated to a common struggle or ideal and serve for the development of certain new thoughts, but for limited scope only. In fact they risk sterility because of narrowness or one-sidedness and therefore are of little import in the wider cultural field.

Even certain outstanding accomplishments in this cultural field, although they seem to contradict this, have never wholly escaped this danger. This is shown by their impact having been restricted to selected groups only. Since it was felt by only a select few, this very limitation proved the lack of wholeness. There are, of course, certain isolated works of merit beyond the charged field of polarity; but, again, there is no totality. The force of polarity has been the support of all the epochs of great cultural achievement. The outstanding period of German genius, for instance, corresponds to the Ottonian[5] which was in turn the most impressive of German history as far as the influence of woman was concerned, even though it was exercised by only a few women who belonged to the royal families. Feminine influence was of a very different kind at the height of the medieval period when it was felt in every phase of morality and culture. Walter von der Vogelweide with his distinction between "Minne" and "High Minne" lyric song is its immortal witness. However here, too, feminine influence is limited to specific social strata. Nevertheless such periods as are receptive to feminine influence always manifest high cultural achievement while periods of pointedly masculine emphasis immediately become subject to decay.

---

[5] Of the Holy Roman Empire.

39

On the other hand, of course, occasional periods of decadence make temporary limitations understandable as, for instance, the all but heroic times help us appreciate the so-called leagues of men which denoted the distinct emergence of the masculine pole, and in this attitude expressed an aversion to the effeminate man as well as to the masculine woman. That a league of men cannot supply higher standards of culture is obvious; but it can bring about a turning away from certain phenomena that no longer are useful as polar forces of culture. One of the principal obligations of the present age, therefore, is to open up new potentialities for culture on the strength of a new point of view on the part of man as well as on the part of woman.

The potentialities should first of all coincide with natural conditions: with marriage, friendship, and with common associations in various fields. Beyond this one also should face the task of a renewed social companionship. It is in this particular realm, which today has become so sterile, that the strength of the period of German genius became manifest. It is imperative to find anew the indissoluble connection between the form and the formation of life, and to understand that the cultural significance of companionship inheres in the meeting of man and woman on the spiritual plane. It is the expression of such a spiritual intercourse when Herder[6] writes of his meeting with Angelika Kaufmann[7] in Rome, and describes her as "one of the silent, modest graces conveying a harmony of feeling that lifted up the whole of nature and society."

Thus the essential aspect of that which is womanly is by its very nature determined from the vantage point of both beholder and beheld, and the potentialities extend through all the spheres of human existence. Dante's Beatrice and Strindberg's demoniacal feminine personalities, beyond the abyss that separates them, represent the same totality of being, whether

---

[6] Johann Gottfried von Herder, German poet and philosopher (1744–1803).
[7] Swiss painter.

40

plunged in light or darkness, whether on the way to Paradise or to damnation. This indicates that the mystery of charity between man and woman may also be distorted into a mystery of iniquity. However, even though distorted, in the sphere of creative culture it still signifies fertility; but the product of such fertility bears a destructive character.

In this fact comes to light the enormous responsibility that results from the relations between man and woman. To see it solely in the light of a generation and of morals is to grasp this responsibility only by half. That which applies to a new living being in the biological sense is true also of the life being produced by a new artistic or spiritual creation. It is at this focal point that the full share of responsibility of woman as far as culture is concerned emerges. Her image as reflected in the creative work of man, whether in its exaltation or in its debasement, is the very image that she herself presents to him.

The sum total of our considerations thus far shows how our approach to the problem of woman in our time requires qualification. Our point of departure was a culture that in its tangible forms is masculine. The essence of culture, however, is the essence of all life, and it is therefore bound to the laws of all living, to the combined activity of the powers of polarity permeating all creation. It is precisely under this aspect that the essence of culture as spiritual life can be defined.

When the creative artist grasps the wide expanse of cultural manifestations and fashions philosophy, poetry, sculpture, even culture itself, in unison with the language of cultured nations, in allegorical feminine figures, then the womanly aspect against the objective background of the reality of life becomes evident to man, even though veiled, as the concept of the co-operation of woman, in all these creative realms. This indicates that in these domains, consciously or unconsciously, man is related to the totality of being.

It is significant, on the other hand, that in cultural endeavors, where the struggle is keen, doctrinaire premises come to the fore which are articulately masculine, such as materialism, socialism, futurism. It is as though man, when he formulated these terms, knew they applied to his very own sphere only, and therefore named them so as to denote their relation to his own gender. Perhaps it is from this perspective that creative culture in the sense of something that is alive can be determined clearly. It is obvious that in its real fullness it unfolds itself in the places where it continues to include the fullness of existence, where the mystery of charity is still experienced and accepted. Beyond it, obviously, there are still astonishing achievements, but they are closer to another order of things. They are no longer in the fullest sense organic creations from a totality of polaric powers; but here the great stream of culture, tumbling in cascades as it were, begins to rush toward the shores where mysteries are no longer needed, and the last remnants of culture end in mere civilization.

This leads to a further insight. The presence of the feminine element means, as we have seen, that of a hidden influence, a helpful, a co-operating, a ministering one. The impulse of reverence belongs to woman. To determine the boundaries of a living culture by the presence of the mystery of charity is to do so by means of reverence, and the motif of reverence is but another name for the veil motif.

In civilization however, the motif of reverence is not so transparent as the motif of willful domination. Civilization does not know of co-operation; it merely makes enchained and soulless powers serviceable. The boundaries of culture, then, as traced by the absence of the womanly element, coincide necessarily with the line where the absence of the religious element begins.

The religious element, as said before, does not mean the divine as such, but it denotes reverence for the divine, and therefore, first of all, humility. The modern world wants none of this virtue because it considers it the epitome of unworthiness. This, of course, is a misconception. The opposite of humility is not dignity but pride, which is an exaggeration of the true dignity of a man and therefore makes him unworthy of his very calling. Humility on the other hand is the expression of the innate dignity of man in the presence of God. So far as creativeness is concerned, the religious quality expressed as humility is meant to help us understand how all accomplishments of man on the natural level are for those who have a supernatural faith.

The sovereign creative qualities of man are but one aspect of creation; the other is humility. The dawning of the other dimension of existence is at bottom the dawn of the humility of the creature. It is the essential condition for the dawning upon man of God the Creator, the God who inexorably works from the two spheres of being at one and the same time. In the co-operation of woman as the mate of his spirit, man experiences his own creativeness as mere co-operation in the work of God, who alone is the real Creator.

Only in this connection is our reference to the anonymous element in every truly great cultural accomplishment understandable. We spoke of this before. If the names of the great architects of our romanesque cathedrals are for the most part unknown to us, and if we can no longer recognize the figure of the builder behind his work, this does not by any means indicate only that their period was lacking in a sense of personal tradition. It denotes primarily the consciousness that every great work, even in its transcendental aspects, contains an added element of mystery that extends beyond its natural creator.

As all these cathedrals were built for God's glory alone, so at the same time, in the consciousness of their builders, they were built by God. Before man was able to build them, God had produced their image in the mind of man. In the anonymity of these great builders, man as it were follows in the footsteps of woman and before God becomes as nameless as woman. In this anonymity he finds reflected the other side of his creativeness, and we begin to recognize in the surpassing magnificence of these cathedrals the real and ultimate meaning of anonymity. If

43

hitherto it appeared as a collaborating element, it here discloses itself also as a co-creative one.

The sublimity of these cathedrals reveals the mystery by which creation proclaims God's creative power on the one hand, and on the other conceals it. God is hidden, a silent, an invisible God. In His creation, He remains in a sense anonymous. This helps us to understand, as we just said, that the power which collaborates also co-creates. Woman, therefore, as the hidden collaborator, represents the anonymity of God; she represents it as the one side of all that is creative. Man, however, participates in this quality in so far as he assumes the function of woman, for only in the working together of both the anonymous and the perceptible forces is the totality of creativeness consummate.

The tremendous meaning of the anonymous which our time has readily recognized along secular lines, not only emanates from the religious concept, but is actually rooted in it. Once more, and in its most profound sense, the dual character of the mystery of charity becomes apparent at this point, and the reason why it rests equally upon the nuptial Mass and the consecration of the virgin becomes obvious: the bride of man is called in like manner to be the Bride of Christ.

By the same token the meaning of the anonymous element in creative culture hinges upon the religious significance of woman. This is what Léon Bloy expresses with the words: "*plus une femme est sainte, plus elle est femme.*" This is to say: "the holier a woman is, the more she is a woman." This also is Dante's meaning in that wondrous passage of his great poem when he looks upon Beatrice while her eyes remain steadfastly fixed upon God. Here Dante does not see the divine in woman; but he sees God because her glance is upon God. This is the religious significance of woman and at the same time the meaning of the love between man and woman, recognized and portrayed in its ultimate depths. Here the symbol of the mirror, which so often appears in poetry, rises to its highest potentiality.

Woman who along the horizontal level of her earthly existence denotes the unity of all creation, on the higher plane signifies also the glance toward the Creator. Totality in a natural sense reaches out beyond itself toward the totality of the supernatural.

The masculine element alone, even the human element by itself, does not suffice. Only in the collaboration of God and man does that ultimate and all-embracing totality appear which is the prerequisite of every masterpiece. That which applies to the single cultural achievement must naturally be true also of culture in its entirety.

This eliminates the second assumption of our preliminary considerations. The religious element is not, as we then assumed, a powerless one; it is, on the contrary, the concealed strength of all culture.

From this it follows inescapably that there is no cause that contributes so much to the downfall of culture as an exclusive dependency on temporal values only. The more closely culture is identified with these ephemeral values, the faster it will sink to the level of mere civilization. A comparison with the creative works of the past shows clearly what culture is when religious, and what it is when irreligious. The staggering disparity between the work of Dante, Cervantes, Shakespeare, or even that of Goethe and Kleist, and contemporary literature of the past few decades, is due not so much to a deficiency of talent among modern writers as it is to the fact that their talents lack the vision of that farther horizon which is developed only in a climate conducive to their healthy growth. For this reason their development entails the obligation of overcoming standards of culture which are totally without a higher purpose and therefore unbearably inadequate.

Talents can be made to grow, but they can also wither away. When the substance has reference to totality, it yields inevitably the breadth and the greatness that give a totality of form as well. The actual paradox of culture comes to light when it is self-seeking and one-sidedly worldly, for then it decays. It reaches out

45

beyond itself and attains to eternal values which make it a partner in the realm truly its own when it has religious motivation.

From this dual totality it follows, furthermore, that the betrayal of the mystery of charity is always twofold. Its twofold aspects are inextricably interwoven. The creative personality who no longer gives God the honor, and instead proclaims only himself and excludes the religious element from culture, practically must also eliminate its womanly quality. In making only his own demands upon culture, man tears the totality of existence to pieces, immanently as well as transcendentally.

In this connection it is evident why the decline of culture is always closely linked with moral decay. Marital infidelity and divorce appear but as an expression of separation between man and woman, and are directly related also to their spiritual separation; not only because they undermine art (as just one instance) with elements of disintegration, but in a much more profound sense. Marital infidelity symbolizes and divorce legalizes the betrayal of the mystery of charity. When man makes exclusive claims upon culture he rejects as it were the bride of his spirit in the same manner as he deserts his wife by infidelity and divorce. Henceforth he stands alone, while culture enters a phase of ominous and sterile separations which in our day are branded as individualism because their deepest roots are not seen. The isolation of the individual which rightfully is deplored and condemned, is but the result of a fundamental cleavage in the world, the last slow beat, in a sense, of a tidal wave of immeasurable range.

For cultural life, then, the absence of the feminine half of existence has an import similar to that which heresy means for the Church. Heresy is always the outcome of one-sidedness and isolation. By substituting a part for the whole and making that part absolute it distorts the truth. Again the image of the Eternal Woman becomes visible at this point as though it were cast over the destiny of woman in time: Mary, according to the

46

teaching of the Church the conqueror of heresy, stands for the restoration of that totality which corresponds to the will of God, by way of the mystery of charity.

During the epochs when a one-sided, masculine culture prevails, not only are all feminine characteristics absent, but faith in the hidden forces is then replaced by a reliance on bare visibility, as shown either in naked violence or a blatantly revealing publicity. Such a culture means, furthermore, an excess of masculine characteristics, and their disfigurement in the very face of the man who stands alone. The absence of one part of reality, and this is extremely important, calls forth a strange unsteadiness in the image of the other part.

"Only when I am most completely yours, am I entirely my own," Michelangelo writes in his sonnets to Vittoria Colonna. The exaggeration of masculine traits in cultural pursuits expresses negatively the validity of these words. Every image has its meaning and its mission only within the totality. The very epochs which exclude woman from their cultural life in reality manifest in a negative but nonetheless impressive fashion their own special need of her. Consequently, the elimination or suppression of woman in man-made plans never represents the real misfortune, for in such instances only questions of fact and not of essence are at stake. Even the rejected wife retains her nuptial character and is, in her banishment, immeasurably significant. As wife she retains her position in the eternal order of woman's life as the other half of man. It is then that the sacrament of matrimony, as the highest form of the mystery of charity and its actual consecration, stands forth in its unimpairable sublimity and in the fullness of its sacred character, precisely when the marriage is most endangered.

The divorced woman remains a wife and the other part of the man, because she retains this dignity before God. It is in the indissolubility of sacramental marriage that the importance of the sexes as polaric forces in the universe comes to the fore. Metaphysically considered, this indissolubility denotes the in-

47

separability of the two correlated spheres of being, and the primal fact that God has established the one half of existence as irrevocably feminine.

Man's rejection of woman, however, never comes about without woman having her share of responsibility for it. Far worse than the man who desecrates the spiritual mystery of charity is the woman who disrupts the divine orders of feminine life. In this respect the beginning at the turn of this century of the equal rights movement was rather revealing. Clearly the struggle for woman's suffrage was the result of the dissonance that had come about in feminine nature. The religious bond cementing the family was widely destroyed and as a result the specific sphere of woman was badly upset. This sphere had still offered the possibility for an absolute fulfillment even to the unmarried woman so long as the perspective toward ultimate values remained unimpaired.

The feminist movement had its spiritual roots in the dullness and the narrowness of the middle-class family. Its economic backgrounds do not concern us here. From the stress of their starving souls, the women of that period cried out for a spiritual purpose in life and for an activation of their capacity for love. It was a tragic motivation, for these women sought a share of responsibility in the man's world, and sought it outside the family which could no longer shelter and satisfy them.

To the dull and narrow-minded middle-class family corresponded a national and an international family which, through the dissolution of the religious bond, had likewise been largely destroyed. This destruction coincided with new and unheard of obligations arising because of the need to make both material existence and culture secure. The woman of that time, ready to help, plunged into this caldron of distress and struggle which affected both bodies and souls because it was the result of a loss of balance, spiritually no less than materially, of both the individual and the masses. From the experience of her own needs, woman found her way to the universal need, and learned to appreciate the importance of participation in social responsibility. This will remain forever as a page of honor in her history.

Like almost every great and vital thought of the present day, this idea of sharing responsibility is a Christian heritage. We saw before that the idea of the vicarious is originally sacred in character. When viewed in this perspective, even though scarcely perceptible, the positive, truly womanly impulse that gave rise to the feminist movement becomes evident. At once the reason becomes equally plain why the results of this impulse necessarily remained far behind all hopes and expectations. The fate of the feminist movement represents but a part of the destiny of the epoch. It was bound to be what it was; for, instead of renewing the foundations of society, the efforts simply went in the direction of reinforcing the outer walls of the social structure. The very introduction of the social question as one of an independent category indicates a certain degradation of culture, for only spiritual resources, not merely social means, can regulate the social order.

Instead of tackling the cultural problem under a fundamental perspective, the struggle centered on preliminary and secondary issues. Instead of saving the spirit itself, the leaders of the movement felt obliged primarily to secure only its potentialities. The general distress that woman was facing in the world was caused by the same distress that had driven her out of the family. She could, to be sure, bring her influence to bear upon the solution of spiritual and social problems, but it depended solely upon her attitude toward the eternal order of being whether or not she could make her own specifically feminine contribution to the social family she now entered as she had made it before within the precincts of the home.

Woman can assert her womanly quality only as carrier of the womanly symbol; and her symbol is the veil, the sign of espousal. The cultural role of the woman adhering to the eternal orders is that of bride to the spirit of man. However, the meaning of the eternal orders had already been destroyed and hence the degradation of the intimate union between man and woman necessarily followed upon the disintegration of the whole fabric of spiritual life. Organization replaced the vital interchange of forces. The bond of a mere contract superseded the natural bond that accords with God's will, and negotiation stood in the stead of mystery. The profound realization of being with one another became the workaday experience of being next to one another, where it had not already degenerated into being against one another.

The period of the rising feminist movement went parallel with the adoption of the nonsensical expression, "struggle of the sexes." To make the movement responsible for this would be a total inaccuracy as well as an injustice. This term, however, even where such a battle was not sought and never took place, caused a danger zone to be formed.

To be sure, the real and deepest danger to woman did not arise from a refusal, but in the opposite direction. The veil is not only the symbol of the bride of man, but also of the Bride of Christ. The woman of the period in question was visible, but lastly not effective. This means that even in becoming visible woman must remain the representative of invisible powers. Léon Bloy's words, "the holier a woman, the more she is a woman," are valid also in reverse; for the truly feminine role in every situation is irretrievably bound to her religious function.

The sublime and almost awe-inspiring analogy which the Church uses at a marriage ceremony, the comparison with the union between Christ and the Church, has the profound purpose of making the woman realize that the bride of man should also be the Bride of Christ and actually belongs to God. This alone gives to St. Paul's words that woman should be subject to man their innermost meaning. It is because he exacts this submission in a religious sense, that the inner freedom of the woman in her surrender becomes assured. The consciousness of belonging to God should protect her from herself; for her peril does not lie only in the refusal of surrender, but also in an exaggerated one. The mystery of charity can also degenerate. Whenever woman's union with God has loosened or disintegrated there is danger of woman's exaggerated surrender to man. It is then that her relationship to man also absorbs that which belongs to God. This relationship is determined by the same barrenness, the same absence of a high horizon that we have recognized as deadly in a culture that is only worldly. This latter type of culture reflects only the degeneration of the mystery of charity. Along the entire line of our reasoning, the truth that most vitally concerns our times is that without eternal values we lose not only eternity, but this life as well.

For the woman of the recent past this is to say that the quality which we were inclined to characterize as masculinity in the woman frequently revealed itself upon closer scrutiny as simply an unrestrained femininity. There is a certain type of feminine humility that betrays the man and delivers him to his own pride. The so-called masculine woman represents only a variety of womanhood no longer devoted to man according to the spirit of the divine order. This order, which applies in all places and in every situation where man and woman meet, constitutes the mystery of charity in its profound interchange of giving and taking. Where a womanhood no longer giving itself according to this divine order ends, a womanhood either withholding itself or becoming the slave of man begins.

If we compare the so-called masculine woman with the heroines of the novels of the same period, we can easily discern their similarity. Even the woman of that time who persevered in the family frequently demonstrates the same type. As she lost herself to the man to the point of repugnance and disgust, in an atmosphere of sensuality and emotion, so also along spiritual lines she surrendered herself unreservedly and with a lack of restraint that equaled a betrayal of the mystery of charity and a betrayal as well of her own inherent powers and potentials. She tried to share man's intellectual pursuits, but merely adopted his methods. In the social field she sought opportunities to develop her deepest faculties and allowed herself instead to be inserted as only a link in his machinery. In a doubly fatal way she succumbed as woman to the very one-sidedness, to the mistakes and the dangers which had been the pitfalls of the man of that period. The mistake was not so much inherent in the aims of the feminist movement and in the situations it created as it was due to the character of the epoch, which in its spiritual life no longer knew its true obligations and no longer had a clear objective.

The consequences of this situation soon became obvious and were clearly reflected in the contemporary literature. The novels usually end with hopeless uniformity in the breaking up of love and marriage. The woman who destroys love and marriage always is the counterpart of the man who by infidelity and divorce rejects his wife. In succumbing to man, woman no longer surrenders; she throws herself away. She has nothing more to give, is no longer man's other half. As woman, in a sense, she ceases to be and the balance of life, its polarity, has been destroyed thereby. In clinging exclusively to the pole to which she does not properly belong, she loses the one that is her own; the mystery of charity with its profound reciprocity is wiped out, and with it the fecundity of the relationship.

Woman's exclusion from the spiritual realm of man leads to exactly the same consequences as shown by the collapse of such marriages. What happened in Germany during the flagitious period of the Nazi regime is a case in point, for at that time the significance of woman was blatantly challenged to an extent where the mystery of charity was utterly disregarded and even sneered at. The man who then had usurped the rule of the country was a typical manifestation of that state of mind which simply ignores that there is another half of being, the feminine one. While this writer certainly does not pretend that the responsibility for the Nazi outrage was man's only, and while in its end effect it is even more distressing that women should lend their support to such aberrations than when such support comes from men — nevertheless our contention is not weakened by these sad experiences. However, under the aspect of the mystery of charity the Nazi period was one of the most deplorable of history because it refused to acknowledge that mystery is the only truly creative principle in human life.

Today, of course, the feminist movement has widely achieved its objectives. We no longer face it as a struggle, but must now deal with its results. In many fields of endeavor formerly reserved to man, woman has gained a foothold in a most gratifying way, be it as a teacher, a physician, a lawyer, or as a social welfare worker. Even as a scholar she can point to achievements which deserve respect and gratitude because they amount to a vital supplementation of man's work.

However, all human progress has its tragic drawbacks and so has the progress of the feminist movement. Since it has asserted itself there is a growing lack of available workers in the fields originally woman's. Among the religious communities both Protestant and Catholic, and in the Red Cross, the complaint that there is not enough readiness on the part of women to lend their charitable, typically womanly aid is so universal that it cannot be ignored. At the same time mothers and housewives no longer find the helping hands of women willing to do the work of domestic servants which is so rewarding and so naturally in keeping with woman's calling.

No doubt this explains at least partly the decay of present-day cultural life. No scientist, no artist can accomplish what he sets out to do, if selfless feminine hands do not provide for his material needs. No physician, no matter how gifted, can take care of his patients if good nurses are missing. Social life cannot prosper, no home can be a true refuge, if women do not quietly tend to their duties. Only woman can succeed in counteracting the present-day trend toward anonymity, by breaking up the cold pattern of mere organization which is one of the decisive factors in the plight of modern life. Of course, regarding the facilities and compensation with which the needed woman should be provided, in accordance with present day requirements, a standard equal to that applied to men should be used. We must always remember how many women who formerly could choose their employment in accordance with their personal tastes and preferences, today must look after the needs of impoverished parents and relatives.

There is one conclusion that can be drawn from the widespread absence of modern woman in the positions and professions typically feminine: modern woman is to some extent no longer the one with whom this book is concerned. Is it not of an almost symbolical significance that even the long flowing bridal veil nowadays is so often replaced by the mere allusion of a veil which barely reaches the shoulders? Even a deeply veiled widow we may most likely meet only at an open grave. The pace of modern life and its busyness, also perhaps a certain reluctance to face the serious portent of human existence, no longer allows the wearing of solemn mourning clothes which formerly were considered obligatory for at least one year. Only the nun as the bride of Christ has preserved the veil of marriage even though she seems to become a rarer figure from year to year.

This brings us to the truly tragic aspect which was already apparent in the very beginning of the feminist movement, and which it shares with the over-all trend of our age. It is no longer a secret that Christians by name are numerous, but Christianity as a whole hardly exercises a widely constructive influence any longer. This is demonstrated shockingly by the decrease of humaneness that became obvious in the course of World War II and now becomes even more manifest, with the threat of a third cataclysm overhanging us, which makes the very existence of a Christian sense of responsibility questionable, even in countries where Christian traditions are accepted in principle and sometimes proclaimed obtrusively. Only the unreserved acceptance of the tenets of charity, the love of God and fellow man as Christians are supposed to practice it, even in regard to the enemy under the precepts of the Gospel, can bring salvation. Probably this is the only way to overcome the trend toward atheism. We should remember that the tragedy of Hiroshima has had the consequence of rendering, not Christianity itself, but certainly Christians to a large extent untrustworthy in the eyes of the Eastern people.

This now leads us to consider the image of woman in the light of the proximate as well as the distant future. Clearly there are limitations which always existed. Not only for the present, but very likely forever, woman will be kept from visibly sharing in the determination of the great destinies of nations. In the face of political decisions all women's organizations, no matter how well-intentioned, are bound to fail. Bertha von Suttner, the great Austrian pacifist and Nobel Prize winner, did not succeed in her time. Today her goal seems to be even farther beyond reach. Is it not significant that on the part of women, even Christian women, there is so little evidence of resistance to the threat of annihilation by our modern weapons? When such resistance does become evident, how easily it is ignored!

There are those who say that women would have to control the means of political power, if they were to stem the present-day, horrible tide which menaces the whole world. It is pointed out that only men are in the drivers' seats. However, such an objection is but the expression of an excuse which is not really valid. There is no question of having women engage in political activities directly, as for instance in India. They may do so and again they may not do so. What is decisive in the end is that they deprive man of that power which relates to destruction, or to the threat of destruction. A threat never is a constructive procedure, for it only attacks brutality with brutality. In other words, the objective is to make visible again in the countenance of creative man the image of the spouse, to affirm the other pole of reality. It is in this respect that woman absolutely must act.

The great late Russian philosopher Nicholas Berdyaev has

predicted a role for woman in the near future that would be greater than heretofore. The question is whether woman today can meet such a challenge. What kind of an impression do we gain of the "woman in time" today? Is it of a deeper significance that she has dropped her veil? If this is so, then woman has not accomplished her loftiest mission, despite all the victories she has achieved in public life.

What is it that is missing in this modern world of ours, despite all its outward splendor, its technology and economic progress? It is that minimum of kindness, motherliness, mercy, sense of tact and tenderness which comes from woman as her contribution to the life of man. It is not an official concern of woman with activities that are but preliminary that is at issue, but rather the restoration of the feminine reality in the countenance of a man who seemingly knows no longer of the dignity of the mystery of charity and the obligation it entails. Will woman be able to fulfill Berdyaev's hope?

The image of woman today is to a large extent problematic. The arrogant, brutal predominance of glamorous publicity makes it difficult to gain access to its inner meaning. In public life the flighty movie star, the beauty queen, or some other feminine type that appeals to publicity seekers stands in the very forefront with little sense of discretion. No reporter needs relieve these women of a veil, for they themselves have taken it off in their quest for recognition. The fashion makers, guided as they are by a natural nonchalance which must be welcomed within limits, and being free of outworn conventional moods, no longer are interested in what used to be called the charm of the décolleté, but insist on having woman undress herself as much as possible, and on exposing her in the true sense of the word. Woman's external appearance has become a product of the beauty parlor which manages to make attractive even those who may be at a natural disadvantage. There would be no reason to object to such practices, if they were not coupled with a virtual elimination of all that is unique in an appearance, the traces of an individual destiny and of the years that have been lived through. Little is to be expected of a woman attracted by the type of advertising which promises success if only proper cosmetics are used, especially if such advertisements stress that these beauty aids will help to make her an object of envy — as though it were not repulsive to incite envy and thus to offend against charity.

However, we should look for deeper motivations in our search for the true image of modern woman. Once before we have tried to gain the proper insight by consulting contemporary literature. These sources again are conclusive in this context, for the destruction of the mystery of charity is evident in modern writing. In its stead the themes are mostly superficial relationships which usually have an ending tragic for the woman, such as divorces and broken marriages which always seem to lead to new ties equally destined to disintegrate. All this literature is dominated by the urge to reflect our era realistically. Effectively it mirrors life as it is actually lived, and no doubt every age has a right to have its image presented in its individuality. The degenerating specific consequences of the last war still shake society and perhaps certain things must be said to be overcome. At the same time the desire to produce the type of writing and poetry which truly reflect the spirit of the times should not make us overlook the unshakable age-old principle that art is to provide each age with its proper medicine. This means it should be its beacon.

An example of such art is the book by Heinrich Boell, small in size, but apt to engage attention, which is entitled "Nobody Said a Single Word." Here we are made aware unpretentiously of the mystery of the spouse who in the midst of blaring publicity and the frenzy of hectic people, strangely hypocritical and slaves of their passions, still represents mystical dignity even though she is abandoned by her husband. She emerges victorious because she remains true to herself. If on the one hand the anguished work of a Frances Sagan gained a sad world-wide reputation for the way it presents a modern image of woman, then on the other hand — unexpectedly because we had not anticipated it coming from that part of the world — there came a witness for womanhood who will remain unforgotten because of his poetic forcefulness. He was Boris Pasternak, the great late Russian writer, who in his master novel has lifted up human love to a level of true grandeur. Against the background of his people's apocalyptic destiny he portrays like a shining promise the love of man and woman which, though externally defeated, remains victorious in the realm of the spirit, as the great mystery on which by divine design rests the polar force of all natural and supernatural life.

Shall we see this prophecy of love come through in our time? We know that today our very existence is at stake, not only our culture. Pasternak's book was written at a time when the human race is struggling to preserve its very life. Once again we are facing a world deprived of woman's healing power. While the conquest of space engages the energies of so many new Argonauts, and consumes unbelievable sums of money, humanity, blinded in a promethean quest, seems bent on preparing the destruction of its very own planet.

It is with these thoughts in mind that we gain the proper perspective for the present age. Evidently at this point the past epoch reaches over into ours. In reality woman today has lost her power as a symbol while she was still believed to be retaining it. Viewed beyond the mere surface, a culture no longer turned toward God with a sense of responsibility for its creation has actually foregone the presence of woman. The woman, however, who recklessly and supinely allows herself to become part of such a culture thereby but approves of her own exclusion. Her presence then becomes a mere pretense. To establish the full weight of the other half of being, woman has one chance and that is to be this other half and to become aware of the primal powers and the original role of womanliness. It is neither the self-will of man nor the willfulness of woman that determines what the womanly vocation really is. Here St. Augustine's magnificent utterance applies: "Love God and do what you will." For the woman who maintains the attitude of the *fiat*, no matter under what circumstances, one might give this thought a new interpretation and yet preserve its essential meaning by saying: Be truly a woman and do what you will.

Woman's way into the future would then appear to be obvious. It should be consonant with Berdyaev's thought in his book *The New Middle Ages*, where he alludes to the role of woman and her important part in the religious awakening of our times. "For the coming historic epoch," he says, "the growing significance of woman has nothing in common with a continuation of the modern movement for the emancipation of women which seeks to lead them along masculine ways. This is an antihierarchic, a levelling movement. . . . It is not the emancipated woman, placed upon an equal footing with man; but it is the eternal feminine, that in the approaching historical period will increase in significance."

The greater significance that Berdyaev predicts for woman, the new significance which these pages also have for their topic, is one that implies the reflection of the womanly quality becoming visible again in the countenance of creative man, in order that the mystery of charity as a divine principle be restored. Only within the framework of this divinely ordained order can man and woman meet one another creatively. This means the re-establishment of the totality of being, of its full abundance and thereby its renewal. If this fails, we face total ruin.

The destruction of the totality of being caused by attributing absolute value to its separate parts instead of attributing it to the whole, always and irrefutably means the destruction of the parts as well as of the whole. The betrayal of the mystery of charity is always a dual one. To disregard woman in her symbolic significance amounts to a disregard of the *fiat mihi* and thereby of the religious element as such. As a rule it results from the pride of the self-assertive man; but it may also be the consequence of woman's denial of her own symbol.

Today both these perils have grown to colossal proportions. Let us not deceive ourselves. A culture that consistently refuses to accept God as its supreme law and objective must ultimately accept Him as its judgment. All eternity has a twofold character in that it represents either the religious fulfillment of time or the fulfillment of time in its apocalyptic meaning; for the Apocalypse is the final form in which a dying culture points beyond itself.

The final Apocalypse of St. John's Revelation is preceded by apocalypses of separate cultural cycles. Here we can deal with only one of these for the whole of creation is beyond reach for promethean man. We should not envision such a limited apocalypse as the lightning splendor of some transcendent tempest of angels. It is only the announcement of the "latter days" that is of visionary magnitude, for their herald is still bound by an eternal mandate which alone makes his prophetic vision possible. If the fulfillment of the prophecies were to strike our own cultural cycle, it would portray in the hugeness of the impact a general destruction of monstrous proportions. An inner view, however, would reveal the utter pettiness of a miserable annihilation.

The war of the Horsemen of the Apocalypse is not the kind of war that might be a man's heroic destiny; nor, as a denial on the part of nature, does famine follow disease and death as the discharging of elemental powers. Rather, it may be the result of mercenary principles that involve no sense of responsibility, or of a scholarship grown godless. We know today that these two evils can cause the loss of entire harvests and the poisoning of whole nations. The woman in time, however, who will be the woman of those latter days is not the great whore of Babel of whom St. John tells, not the demoniacal temptress of recreant kings; but it will be the workaday, petty sort of femininity which abandons God's order. It will be the woman who has ceased to be the bearer of her eternal symbol.

The absence of one part of reality, as we have seen before, always produces unsteadiness in the image of the other part. In its deepest sense, the world of the Four Horsemen is the world without woman. It is not indeed the man's world; for it is a world in which, for him also, the spirit of the *Fiat mihi,* "Be it done unto me," no longer exists, where there is no co-operation of the creature with God. It is the world without God, the world which becomes destructive in character when it tries to depend on human strength alone. A culture that has become incapable of life dies no natural death; it strangles. With the inroad of the Four Horsemen the tragic course of a culture that has grown one-sided from both the immanent and the transcendental point of view continues with inexorable determination. The disintegration of the outer structure of the world but completes the destruction of its foundations.

The scales are still trembling. It seems that the only consolation that woman can give to mankind today is her faith in the immeasurable efficacy of hidden powers, her unshakable conviction that not only a visible but also an invisible pillar supports the universe. When all the earthly potentials shall have exhausted themselves in vain, and in the present crisis of society this seems almost to have happened, then, even for a humanity largely grown godless, the hour of a supreme, eternal calling will strike again. But the divine creative power can emanate from heaven to renew the face of the earth, only if the earth itself responds again with religious fervor, with the readiness of the "Be it done unto me."

The hour when God's help becomes manifest is always mankind's religious hour, the hour of the woman, the hour of the creature's co-operation with the Creator. God grant that woman may not miss her approaching hour! On the fatal way between heaven and hell which humanity treads today, the same guides to whom Dante long ago entrusted himself on his own risky path are needed. By means of the poet's and the seer's vision of all the hells and purgatories of this life we find the way to Paradise only when we meet the loving woman whose eyes rest in God. The greatest poem of all times is both the most supernaturally sublime revelation and the eternally valid proof of the creative meaning of the mystery of charity.

TIMELESS WOMAN

Sadly do we recall today the year 1900 when Ellen Key's great book on *The Century of the Child* first came out. What happened to *The Century of the Child*? How much suffering did the children experience during its course! How much brutality did two world wars and famines cause these innocent little ones to undergo, and how great are the dangers they face again in our very day! While charitable boys and girls towns and other institutions of a similar kind are established, and a great deal is being done to help the youngsters, the complaint of the loneliness of youth becomes more articulate all the time, for children are all too often left to themselves while their mothers go to work instead of providing them with the kind of homes which were lifelong sources of physical and moral strength for them in previous generations. A deep shadow is being cast by these trends upon our vaunted and all too proud age, for the intense distress and loneliness of youth shows that motherhood and motherliness are no longer what they were in former times: the natural fulfillment of womanhood. This naturally implies at the same time the possibility that true motherliness is no longer properly understood.

The danger is in fact quite evident. It is only the city dweller spending his weekends in the country who goes into raptures about nature; the farmer breathes in it. It is only the sterile critic who is given to much talking about art. For the artist himself, his art is speech sufficient. It is only a motherless time that cries out for a mother, and a deeply unmotherly age that can point to the mother as a demand of the time; for it is precisely the mother who is timeless, the same in all epochs and among all peoples.

In a mother's countenance which knows of no age the differing destinies of queen and beggar woman lose their contrast. The distinguishing characteristics of nations and the disparities between primitive and highly developed levels of culture vanish in her presence. Motherhood can never become for woman the special task of a certain time; for it is her very own task. The mother as such does not bear the individualizing marks of the person, nor does she carry the stamp of an epoch. With her every seasonal program ends, for time itself has no power over her. Under the form of virgin she stands solitary in the face of time, as bride she shares time with the man who lives in it, as mother she conquers time.

On earth the mother is the image of endlessness; centuries pass over her joy and her sorrow and leave no trace behind. She is ever the same, the boundless abundance, the silence, the immutability of life itself, in its power of conceiving, of bearing, of bringing forth. In this she is comparable only to the fertile womb of the earth which likewise we cannot urge, except within limits, to pour its blessings upon us; for in all the things that concern essential and original life, man's power of will and action never extends farther than the foreground.

The motif that is basic to all that comes to pass through woman is fundamental also to woman's function of giving birth. The veil that the bride wears on her wedding day is not only the symbol of her inviolate virginity; it is symbolic also of the marriage upon which she is to enter. The same veil that conceals the bride enfolds also the cradle of her child. This is the profound meaning of the beautiful custom of carrying the child to baptism under the mother's bridal veil. Conception and birth are the hour and the mystery of life, which means that they are the hour and the mystery of woman.

It is this trait of mystery that Ruth Schaumann[1] points out in her letter, *Chelion to Cletus*, when she writes: "True women are quiet and desire quiet. . . . Show me the woman who writes

---

[1] Distinguished German Catholic poet and artist.

about that which concerns her intimately. . . . If it did concern her she would be silent; for here silence is life; speech, death. . . . The mystery always bears fruit; but its revelation means its end." Here Ruth Schaumann refers not only to the impact of our times upon the timeless woman. If we survey the past decades in a glance, it becomes evident that the stirring cry for the mother reverberating through the present age expresses not so much the impact of the times upon the realm of the timeless woman, as it does the horror of the times at this intrusion. Its portentous beginnings lie in the past. Not only do the public utterances and discussions of the last epoch about "The Right of Motherhood" and "The Cry for the Child" (as in the days of Ellen Key and during the atrocious Nazi period in Germany) point to the danger of marriage and motherhood being undermined, but they actually constitute such a danger. They do it even where they have been inspired by the best of intentions, and the tragedy of it is that this is exactly where they prove how total was the lack of understanding for the specific domain of the maternal woman, nay, of woman herself.

When viewed from this angle, novels and dramas of the period that were based on married life appear in a highly doubtful light. Obviously, marriage, like every great, universally human theme, must be available as subject matter of genuine art, but art also must respect the boundaries of the silence that belongs to the inward reality of things. This does not mean, as the past epoch objected, to limit art in its creative function; but it does mean that art also must follow the only possible way of drawing close to the heart of things. Tragedy in marriages, taken both as a whole and individually, can be remedied only by having regard for this necessary inner domain, and its portrayal in literature is not truly feasible, if this reservation is not respected.

It is true that both these points of view were extremely difficult for a time like the past epoch to accept, accustomed as it was always to focus its hopes only upon that which it undertook, carried on, and discussed with an activity that was visible far and wide. In this respect our own time is still largely in alignment with the past. This is particularly evident in the call for the mother now again so noticeable. This appeal, although altogether justified, nevertheless denotes a fundamental and an absolute helplessness. In all the things that concern the essence and origin of life, the volitional and the active powers of man never penetrate beyond the foreground. Our times have recognized correctly the dangers to motherhood that come from the self-love and degeneration of woman. In most cases the elemental mother nature that is in her would prevail; it would also be able to tear the fetters imposed upon her by economic necessity, were it not that nature itself already is in chains.

A fettering of the natural forces that threaten man always means a restriction also of the natural potentials of man. We must realize that even the most beneficial form, such as modern medicine and hygiene, in which the inroad of the times into the domain of timeless woman expresses itself, is after all an encroachment. It constitutes the positive side of an enormous technical transformation of the natural functions of motherhood in all their various aspects. The advantage that the future mother derives from the clinic, for her own health and that of her child, is purchased at the expense of tearing away the mystery of birth not only from the shared experience of the family which constitutes the original and natural shelter for the mystery, but also from the awesomeness of the primal powers that are its carriers.

The reverence for nature, which the demand of today for the natural destiny of woman presupposes, depends necessarily upon the degree to which nature may still be regarded as absolute mistress. The disappearance of respect for the sovereignty of nature becomes understandable at once as an attending circumstance of man's technical mastery of nature, if we become aware not only of the positive application of present-day scientific methods but also of their negative aspects. The improved opportunity of preserving the life of the child is paralleled by the equally improved opportunity of preventing or even removing the child. Consequently, today we are dealing no longer with woman in reality subservient to the great, unfathomable forces of nature to whom she should minister with reverence. In her place we have the woman whose timeless character is protected yet hard pressed on all sides by the powers that be; insured, yes, but also infringed upon by them. We must have all this in mind if we would grasp the startling import of the call of today for the mother.

For this reason the demand that we revert to the genuine concept of motherhood in its more profound meaning cannot by any means be regarded as identical with an examination of the status of the individual mother of the present day. Rather, we are concerned with the manifestation of the mother quality in its innermost nature independently of individual motherhood; thus rendering visible, above all temporal limitations, the true countenance of the timeless woman. Herewith we shall find ourselves once more upon the terrain of great art.

At once something remarkable becomes evident. For the image of the mother, supremely great art for the most part makes us depend on that which it conceals. Great drama, especially, withholds almost all information regarding the mother. In *King Lear* Shakespeare has portrayed the tragedy of the father; that of the mother is missing. We have only the outcry of Constance in *King John*; and in *Coriolanus* the two mothers merely stand in contrast to the masculine protagonist. The aged mother is there simply to show that a mother desires to become effective and to receive honor only through her son; while the young mother is addressed "My Lovely Silence." Does the moving beauty of this wondrous title express what Ruth Schaumann has in mind with regard to the individual woman when she writes: "If it concerned her she would be silent"?

Does this silence mean, then, in a deeper sense, that art also knows about the mother? Much could be said for this in so far as great dramatic art is concerned. Every genuine drama revolves around the hour of heroism. Woman's heroic hour, unlike that of man, is not the revelation of an accomplishment widely visible; it fulfills itself rather in profound retirement. As woman recedes from the public gaze, so she withdraws herself from being dramatized. But there is another aspect yet to be considered. Dramatic art is inspired not only from heroic action, but also from the individual performance in its own environment, in accordance with its own laws. The mother, however, is not an individual figure, and she has no law of her own. Her law is the child, and whatever is centered elsewhere is more or less irrelevant to her.

The mother is the timeless woman, for she is not susceptible to change. Her love does not develop. From the first moment it is there. Mother love cannot be really improved since this would imply that once it was less great. Development does not determine the various periods of a mother's life, but these periods are like the lapse of the seasons. Spring and autumn are not developments; they are parts of an unending cycle.

As at the hour of birth the mother stakes her life without reserve for the child, so after its birth her life no longer belongs to herself but to the child. The timeless woman is she who has become engulfed in the stream of the generations; the maternal woman is the one who has submerged herself in the child. Of her Friedrich Hebbel[2] writes:

> She has borne a child
> To loftiest joy and deepest grief,
> And now she is completely lost
> In its mute loveliness.

The natural and immeasurable love that emanates from the mother, and as it were constitutes the shelter within which the child grows to its stature as a person, means for the mother surrender and sacrifice to the point of placing her own stature and her own personality in jeopardy. This again must be understood in a thoroughly heroic, and yet not at all in a pathetic

[2] Nineteenth century German poet.

68

sense. As the heroic hour of birth occurs behind the curtain, so the heroism of the mother's life is accomplished in utter unpretentiousness. The nursery replaces the room of her heavy hour, while she who has passed life on into endlessness fulfills her own living in an unending succession of little and infinitesimal cares. As the mother's heroism is linked with silence, so also is it bound to that which is average and ordinary.

This means that the art form to which the mother is accessible is not the drama, the form of powerful destinies and personalities, but rather the novel, which is the homely art of the everyday. Even as a literary form the novel represents the modest, average qualities that associate themselves with the type of destiny and heroism that belong to the mother. Through its relationship with daily and trivial events, the novel is in a special manner qualified to unfold lovingly the unending trifles that represent a mother's life.

Her really great lines, however, her universal quality, the unpsychological, the immutable, the elemental in her, the part that is so closely bound to nature; in short, her timelessness is not to be found in the time-conditioned art of the novel, but rather in the naïve art of folklore. All that estranges the mother from the drama opens the way to her for the saga and the fairy tale, which do not concern themselves with individual but with typical forms. The mother of the fairy tale is always the same mother. It is especially when she is dead that the fairy tale portrays the unchangeable quality of her love, her inseparability from her child.

In the last resort no fairy tale assumes that a mother could ever die, for death has no power over love or over the immutable. The dead mother of the fairy tale returns at night and rocks her children, or permits nature lovingly to take her place. The mother arms reach out for the orphaned child in the branches of the little tree that has sprung from her grave, and mother hands shower it with gifts. The Breton saga tells of the Berceuse, the woman of death, who whispers into the ears of the dying

69

mariners of sinking ships, lullabies that she had heard their mothers sing. Here the mother of folklore touches upon the deep accord between birth and death.

As nature takes the place of the mother, so the mother represents nature. Sometimes she is felt to be entirely a creature of nature, as in the story of the lovely Melusine. From the profound naturalness with which the fairy tale experiences the mother, comes also its prejudice against the stepmother. Only the genuine mother can be the right one; hence the stepmother, as not appointed by nature, is always evil. The blood relative, however, the sister of the children of the fairly tale, takes the place of the mother who has died, as she does in the story of the *Seven Ravens* and in *Little Brother* and *Little Sister*. As in the fairy tale, so in the folk song the essential mother impulse emerges strongly. The lullaby portrays it by its very form. Through the lips of the mother, expressing all her tenderness and all her love, it sings to the child alone.

As the mother is not a subject for the drama, neither is she in the true sense a theme for sculptural art. That which personality means to drama, form means to sculpture. Personality is a solitary thing while form possesses contour. But the form of the mother is not sharply outlined. It coincides with the form of the child. As in literature it is the novel, the song, the fairy tale, so among the fine arts it is painting which is the medium particularly destined to present the mother and child, for it is the art, not of form, but of color. It is no mere accident that the figures of mother and child are entirely absent from Greek art. So pictorial a subject matter was naturally resistant to the highly developed sculptural feeling of classical antiquity. It was left to Christianity to represent mother and child in sculptural form, but in its sacred connotation. The Madonna is the bearer of the Divine, the torch, as it were, that carries the Light of the world. She is the pedestal of the Child, not a purpose in herself.

Nor does Christian art work out the form of the mother independently; but it places her in a subordinate position, the more to reveal in her quiet posture the enchanting quality of motherhood. The loveliness of the Madonna's face is but the symbol of this inner beauty. Thus the impossibility for art to fashion her as standing alone follows from the very essence of the mother's nature, and the artist can do it only in separating the mother from the child. The genuine mother figure of sculpture is therefore the Sorrowful Mother, the Mother under the cross of her Son. That which breaks the mother to the very depths of her nature makes her a proper subject for plastic art. For this reason also, ancient sculpture, while ignorant of the image of mother and child, still knows the figure of Niobe.

This again throws light upon the relationship between dramatic art and the mother. Her figure, detached from that of the child, is not only that of the mother of a dead son, but it may also be that of a degenerate mother. Once more sculpture and drama are subject to the same law. The rending of the mother from the child makes her an independent figure and therefore capable of dramatic treatment. Of this Medea is the most outstanding example. The Jocasta of *King Oedipus* and the Queen in *Hamlet* also belong to this category. In both these characters degeneration appears as resulting from the predominance of the erotic over the maternal quality. This group includes also Krimhild of the *Nibelungenlied*, dramatically conceived, although in epic form. She is probably the most unmotherly figure in all literature. In the bloody revenge for the death of her husband she sacrifices not only her brothers, but even her own child. With gruesome yet poetic magnificence, this most powerful figure in German literature shows that not every woman who has a child is a mother.

At this point, under the guidance of literature, we are forced, to use the expression of Goethe's *Faust*, to "descend to the mothers" — which means to go beyond the physical mother, to search for the mother in the mother herself. In accord with this thought, the great Nordic writer, Sigrid Undset, has something to say in her novel: *Ida Elisabeth.*

71

The very first pages of this book sound the theme where a young girl says: "When we see how egotistic many people become through family ties, we can readily imagine that God would, if only for the sake of compensation, select a few and allow them to be all things to all." Ida Elisabeth, the heroine of the story, who is entirely disposed toward motherhood in its natural sense, abruptly rejects this idea of being all things to all. She has the misfortune of being married to a man of infantile character, and is obliged to work not only for his support, but also for that of his parents, brothers and sisters.

"Women," she says, "who have the feeling that they are here to bear children, hate and despise it when grown men come and force them to be as mothers also to them." Ida Elisabeth separates from her husband in order to provide a better livelihood for her two little sons to whom alone she feels bound by a mother's duty. Only then does the real issue of her maternal life arise. In her children she draws the unsolved problem of her marriage along with her. From the consideration of her children begins her contact with a man of full stature whom she loves and wishes to marry. However, the children bear the heritage of their immature father. As in the first marriage the inferiority of her husband, so now the superior endowment of the man she loves becomes the problem of her destiny. The question now is not whether, by a second marriage, she can unite husband and children; but whether she will be able to bring into accord this man of character and the children who are marked with the stamp of their inadequate father. In short, the problem of the book is: Does this motherly woman owe herself to the strong man or to the weakling?

In the light of this alternative a decision slowly matures in Ida Elisabeth's heart and she understands that she need not sacrifice for her children's sake her betrothal to the man she loves. One of the finest features of the novel, some of its most ingenious artistry, lies in the avoidance of this very idea of sacrifice. Ida Elisabeth's decision results without any reflection, and is reached beyond her own thinking; it emerges from the depths of her maternal nature. The decision is nevertheless absolute and carries all its consequences within itself. This becomes evident when again she meets her husband who in the meantime had become seriously ill. She no longer refuses herself to him and his family. The mother in her has conquered throughout; her decision is not in favor of the man who is strong, but of those who are weak.

To be a mother, to feel maternally, means to turn especially to the helpless, to incline lovingly and helpfully toward everything on earth that is small and weak. Therefore the principle of motherhood is a dual one. It hinges not only on the birth of the child, but also on fostering and protecting that which has been born. To become a mother physically means but the first eruption of the powers of maternity; it is only the first stirring symbol of something that is much more universal. Her own children lead Ida Elisabeth to the realization that the maternal woman cannot remain the mother only of her own children.

Not only is the child born through the mother, but the mother also is born through the child. "It is the children who awaken us, who say: 'How hard you are; become gentle!' " So Ruth Schaumann writes in her book entitled Yves. The child that at its birth breaks through its mother's womb, breaks through her heart also, opening it to all that is small and weak.

As the face of the Madonna of the Mantle in a wayside shrine emerges through the darkness of the forest, so in Sigrid Undset's novel, amid a thicket of problems such as are debated by our age, the thought arises that a mother is really the mother of all. In Ida Elisabeth's husband and his family an extreme case is described, but that which applies to them, in the final issue, applies everywhere and always. The world has need of the motherly woman; for it is, for the most part, a poor and helpless child. As man comes feebly into the world, so in profound weakness he departs from it; to the hand that wraps the child in its infant clothes corresponds the merciful hand of the woman who supports the aged and wipes the sweat from the brows of the dying. Between birth and death lies not only the achievement of the successful, but the unending weariness of the way, the workaday monotony, all that belongs to the needs of the body and of life.

The motherly woman is appointed the quiet stewardess of this tremendous inheritance of necessity and distress. Under this aspect of mother, woman does not represent, as she does as bride, only the one half of reality. Here her part is much more than half. People know why the man calls his wife "Mother." In doing so he does not address only the mother of his children, but the mother of everyone, which means above all, the mother of her own husband.

It is the mother who prepares his meals, sets his table, mends his clothes, bears his inadequacies, his anxieties, his difficult hours. "The heart of her husband trusteth in her and he shall have no need of spoils," says the Bible in praise of the valiant woman. "And she hath risen in the night and given a prey to her household. . . ." The mother of the man is the mother of all his household. This mother, too, is always the same. Like the mother of the child she can be compared only to the bountiful earth that gives and bears and gives and bears again; and finally, by very reason of this humble earthliness she overcomes the bond of earth. It is the motherly woman, overwhelmed as she is by the needs of every day, who lastly is the great conqueror of the every day. Daily she conquers it anew by making it bearable, and her victory is greatest when least observed.

The man who is engaged in intellectual pursuits exerts himself to overcome materialistic influences and he can succeed only when the motherly woman actually clears them away. The unpretentiousness of this daily victory, its complete obscurity, is the real and innermost glory of the timeless woman, comparable only to that of the unknown soldiers of two world wars. They are the sons of the unknown woman.

In addition to the physical needs of life come the heavy trials

74

that burden the mind and spirit of human beings, the enormous weight of sorrows and crosses, of inadequacy and guilt of all kinds which, in the majority of cases, cannot be removed and must simply be borne. As the motherly woman feeds the hungry, so also does she console the afflicted. The weak and the guilty, the neglected and the persecuted, even the justly punished, all those whom a judicial world no longer wishes to support and protect, find their ultimate rights vindicated in the consolation and the compassion that the motherly woman gives. For her the words of Antigone will always be valid: "Not to hate, but to love with you, am I here." This does not mean to set up weakness as against strength. Quite the contrary. The Bible does not sing the praise of the weak woman, but of the strong one. In the words of the Book of Proverbs: ". . . the law of clemency is on her tongue." It is patience that is strength in the highest degree.

One of the privileges of the maternal woman is the quiet, extremely important function of knowing how to wait and be silent, the ability sometimes to overlook, indulge in, and cover up a weakness. As a work of mercy this is no lesser charity than clothing the naked. It is one of the most ominous errors of the world, one of the most essential reasons for its lack of peace, to believe that all that is wrong must always be uncovered and condemned. Every wise and kindly mother knows that sometimes it is right to do exactly the opposite.

The quotation from the Bible cited above: ". . . the law of clemency is on her tongue," follows the words: ". . . she hath opened her mouth to wisdom." This wisdom often consists in but a pleasantry or a friendly word. In this, too, the woman is veiled. Her wisdom does not manifest itself as something overwhelming, but unobtrusively, and therein lies its greatness. This does not mean to relegate the masterly and judicial wisdom of the man to a secondary place, but it does signify the admission that such wisdom is but one side of the truth. To the very man who would contest this verity, the world would become unbearable if the motherly woman were to fail in making her own specific contribution by such wisdom of her own. Even the man who grudgingly or without understanding accepts it, draws a strength from it that makes life more bearable for him. It is often the last resource of patience, kindness, and forbearance, without which all existence, be it of the individual or of nations, is in danger of becoming a hell. This is the general if not the fully Christian sense of the lovely legend of St. Elisabeth's miracle of roses. It is the simple legend of a woman's motherliness.

Just as the miracle of roses continues to repeat itself, so also does the protest of the landgrave, her husband. Woman's universal motherhood, her absolute relationship to the small and weak, necessarily includes the question of the meaning or the justification of the small and weak things of the world. Man is willing to acknowledge them only under the form of something capable of growth, and this takes us to the second problem in the novel *Ida Elisabeth*, the problem that lies in the distinction between two worlds, that of the man and that of the motherly woman. The following quotation introduces the subject: "Must we not judge the good that is in human beings, as we would a vein of ore when we ask whether or not it is rich enough to warrant the labor spent upon it?"

Doubtless, Ida Elisabeth's husband is one of those who are not worth the effort, who is a plain failure. This is to define a condition as unalterable; it means that here the laws of growth or progress no longer apply. But does this mean an end of the duty of being motherly? With this question the novel enters upon its concluding stage. Plainly it is a matter of the value or the worthlessness of the person as such. At this point the path of the mother and that of the virgin intersect and suddenly we are standing again on the brink of the mystery of all that is imperfect and unfulfilled.

But now, in Sigrid Undset's novel, a wonderful thing happens. The motherly woman, just because of her motherliness, embraces that which has remained fruitless, the incomplete thing,

76

that which, according to earthly standards, is a misfit. At the deathbed of Ida Elisabeth's husband who is a failure we get this message: "Everything by which human beings make something of their lives — love, work, responsibility — these things were and continue to be sufficiently great, now and always; but today a light or a darkness overcasts them, so that the distinctive marks that make one human life different from another have vanished. 'Is it God,' Ida Elisabeth asks, 'in whose hands all the irreconcilable contrasts lie?' And now the face of the dead man gives the answer, 'this radiant, terrifying, this almost triumphant final countenance.' "

Was its inconceivable beauty the image of that which should have been? Was it the sublimity of the thought that the Creator manifests even in a being that apparently has been a failure? Was this beauty the token that the incomprehensible would not always remain incomprehensible? The final evaluation of the human being is not man's prerogative, but belongs to God. According to Sigrid Undset's novel, it is not man who passes judgment, but woman in her motherliness, who, in the face of death, will be found acceptable before God.

One should not forget, however, that in the affairs of this world Sigrid Undset's novel wants masculine influence to be given its full weight, and no less so in regard to the maternal woman. She who must take care of the one who has failed, and must do it with unappraising, unquestioning patience, shares fully in the responsibility for the failure. She is like the wife who, as the bride of man's spirit, carries along with him the responsibility for his cultural work, and the wife who as future mother participates in the responsibility for the child.

It must be clearly understood that in appraising this responsibility we are concerned with only one side of the matter. Man must recognize the reality of this world in its totality, if he wants to fulfill his mission in its regard. He can therefore tolerate weakness only in that which is in process toward maturity, not in that which already is established as an essential reality.

The unconditional motherliness of the woman, on the other hand, that embraces the weakness even in such reality, stands close to the borders of the world beyond. Only in this light does the appraisal of man entail the obligation of acknowledging the maternal world. The miracle of St. Elizabeth's roses signifies the sanction of earthly compassion by eternal mercy.

This gives not only the service of the motherly woman in behalf of weakness but weakness itself its metaphysical meaning. Here we come upon the contingency where the vein of inferior ore nevertheless becomes worth while. Man's limitations are always God's port of entry. The little, the weak, the incompetent ones of the earth are here to make human beings face the reality and need of eternal mercy. They represent human and earthly insufficiency in its gentlest, most appealing form, while its more grievous, more agonizing aspect appears as sin and guilt. Therefore the weak and little ones of the earth not only possess the kingdom of heaven, as the Gospel tells us, but they proclaim it by opening the way to it.

She who cares for and protects the little and weak ones shares in their mission of proclaiming the kingdom of heaven. The words of St. Paul, that the woman should win salvation by the bearing of children, are implemented in the blessing pronounced upon the merciful. If some of the splendor of the happiness and dignity of Mary's motherhood rests upon every maternal woman, then some of it also descends from the crown of the Mother of Mercy.

From this general concept of woman's motherly quality, the correct appreciation of spiritual motherhood follows. This too is a natural power of love, determined by the innate tendency of woman, even when it is not brought to life through a child of her own. This is the motherliness of which the German fairy tale shows an echo in the little sister spinning shirts for the brother ravens who are under a charm; it is the mother quality already present in the child, and surviving in the older woman beyond the hope of physical motherhood. As spiritual maternity is a natural tendency, its unfolding also is a thoroughly natural one. If we said before that physical motherhood is but the first eruption of the mother's powers, their most universal, most appealing aspect, this does not mean that a woman can attain to motherhood in this universal sense only through her own child. It is a remnant of the period of individualism to believe that everyone must experience everything.

The real mother sometimes represents the woman who possesses only spiritual maternity, just as in many instances the woman who is maternal only in a spiritual way must substitute for the woman who has a child but is not in the true sense its mother. In the family it may for instance be the relative or godmother, in public life the guardian, who fills this position. It is not a matter of the destiny of the individual woman, but of her participation in the universal destiny of woman. What matters is the motherliness of every woman, irrespective of external destinies. If Ruth Schaumann in her novel *Yves* says: "She does not know what a mother is; she has never given birth to a child," she refutes this statement in the same book through Germaine who is denied the happiness of motherhood but who takes the strange child to her heart with a mother's love after its own mother deserted it.

Occasionally the stepmother, whom the fairy tale uses so ill, belongs to the category of Germaine, the childless but motherly woman. In Anselm Feuerbach's faithful stepmother she finds herself vindicated. Nevertheless this does not place the fairy tale in the wrong. It knows the depth and the unique quality of the tie that unites mother and child, but it does not know all the potentials of the maternal nature; it does not understand that the spiritual side of motherhood also is a part of nature. The legend, however, does justice to this other mother, and art has represented the Madonna of the childless woman and of the stepmother in Holbein's painting, where the Madonna does not carry the Infant Jesus, but the donor's sick child in her arms.

From this point of view woman's demand for a child of her

79

own appears in a different light. Seen under a spiritual aspect it is not always inspired by the genuine mother instinct. On the contrary, it sometimes reveals a very feminine egoism which leaves but a phantom of the true mother. King Solomon did not allow himself to be deceived by such an allusion. To his wisdom it was the renunciation of the child that gave proof of the real mother. The past decades with their "Cry for the Child" and "Right of Motherhood" have given fatal help in setting up this phantom in place of the real mother.

Indeed, there is no such thing as woman's right to a child; there is only the right of the child to a mother. Ruth Schaumann's words "Only children make us gentle, for they say: 'How hard you are! Become gentle!' " retain their full significance, not only with regard to a child not one's own, but also when there is question of those who may be said to represent the child, the helpless with their arms outstretched, and all those in general who need care and protection. For the woman who is maternal in the spiritual sense, this gives the correct insight into the question of vocation so far as women are concerned. For a woman to be a physician, a guardian, teacher, or nurse is therefore not a profession in the masculine sense of the word, but it is a form of spiritual motherhood.

The past epoch required a profession for the unmarried woman as a substitute for motherhood. The future, inspired by the concept of spiritual maternity, will call for it, but from the totality of motherliness that is also in the single woman. The professions of women are not meant to be the substitute for a missing motherhood, but rather the application of the never failing motherliness that is in every genuine woman.

The decisions whether women should engage in the various professions, and their choice of them, will depend upon the extent to which maternal activity can still be regarded as fruitful. A great number of professions without doubt admit of a purely masculine and a purely maternal interpretation, respectively. In this matter the apparently least feminine of professions, that of politics, is specially instructive. By reason of the universal and spiritual motherhood of woman, when called to the throne to be an independent sovereign she was a good ruler, not in the purely masculine sense of the word, but a good queen, that is, the mother of her people. For this reason in Spain today the memory of the formerly ruling queen has survived the fall of dynasty and form of government. Not only does England remember Queen Bess, and Austria its great motherly empress Maria Theresa, but the Lombardy of today still recalls its Queen Theodolinde.

The woman on the throne is primarily the custodian of her people. The combination of political executive power with maternal prerogatives does not, however, exclude the heroic impulse which is indispensable to political life. Maria Theresa gives proof of this. Even as defender of her people the woman ruler does not lose her maternal quality. She will not wage wars of conquest; but she will defend her people as the lioness does her young. Only when she has betrayed her maternal character has woman in influential political positions been a fatal influence; when, for instance, she acted the part of a Madame Pompadour.

The same applies to the average woman who enters political life. We need not necessarily picture her only as we have seen her in the recent past; for the woman who moves in diplomatic circles or travels abroad has an entirely natural political duty to fulfill, by which she may either help or harm her country. Although in humbler garb than that of queen, the woman in politics is in spirit a mother to her people. Only on this condition can her political activity be approved. No man can replace the voice of a mother; there is question only of how this voice may make its influence felt without distortion.

The realization of the fact that there is no right on the part of the woman to a child, but only a right of the child to a mother, corresponds to the acceptance of another fact that becomes evident for women today, namely, that there is in the world no woman's right, so called, to a profession or vocation;

but the world has a child's right to the woman. If all indications are not deceiving, this right has assumed a highly intensified meaning during the past decades. The cry of today for the mother has its origin not only in desires aroused by problems of population and politics, but its undertone at the same time carries the weight of a spiritual longing. There is nothing that denotes the condition of the world today more profoundly and tragically than the complete absence of the maternal attitude of mind. It means the absence of the sustaining, the bearing, and therefore the fertile forces of life. The impulse alone never suffices; hence we see the terrifying lack of blessing in so many efforts that are in themselves good and useful.

* * *

With these thoughts we have apparently abandoned the topic of timeless woman, but only apparently. In reality we are abandoning rather the consideration of time. The timeless woman is she whom time cannot control; for to surmount time is of the essence of the mother quality. As the woman in giving birth projects life on into endlessness, so in her capacity of nurturing and sheltering life she injects into time an element of eternity.

In connection with her spiritual motherhood, woman's part in culture must be considered once more. In her capacity as a mother she unquestionably becomes the one who protects and fosters cultural values. Unlike her role of wife, by which she supplies an essential half of the reality that enters into the cultural work of man, in her role of mother she is the recipient of this work. The one who receives, however, is usually the one who sustains. We have heard the valiant woman of the Bible praised as the keeper of her husband's goods. Woman also applies her concern for the man's possessions to his intellectual sphere of life. Because of her role of receiving and sustaining, woman has an extraordinarily important part to play in cultural life. Giving without receiving would bear no fruit. It is not due only to the facts that woman often has more time

82

and is more relaxed than man, that she is primarily the one who frequents the bookshop, the concert hall, and the theater, but it is a result of the spiritual destiny of her motherhood. Culture must not only be created; it must likewise be sustained, cherished, even loved like a child. It is but one side, and that the more external, of the fostering of culture if, as today, it is regarded and encouraged largely as the concern of the State. The human element which is of the soul must not be missing and it must come from the love and care that the individual provides.

Once more, then, the orbit of spiritual motherhood dovetails with the realm of physical motherhood. The mother who teaches her child the first words of the language that throughout life will remain his mother tongue, who sings to the child his first native songs and tells him the fairy tales of his people, represents the first determining cultural factor, the earliest spiritual influence in the life of the child. This is of immeasurable importance not only for the child, but for culture as well. The Spanish proverb: "The hand that rocks the cradle rules the world," means first of all that everyone who lives and labors is born of woman. Woman is the mother of the hero and of the saint; she is also the mother of the coward and of the traitor. Surely when the antichrist is born, he will have many mothers. The deeper sense of this world-governing hand, however, consists in the fact that it will continue to lead the son invisibly throughout his later life, and in a hidden way will work with him in the accomplishment of his task.

Woman's part as patroness of culture may also become that of its defender, similar to her position in the political world. She is by nature conservative, which means that she is incapable of destroying that which is faltering. This is an attitude which, in times of upheaval, may be of extraordinary significance. Times of upheaval easily succumb to the danger of surrendering not only outmoded but also timeless possessions. It is here that by reason of her spiritual motherliness woman is primarily called upon to establish a balance. The timeless woman is the keeper of the timeless possessions of her people.

On the other hand there is nothing that contributes so effectively to the downfall of culture as the decline of woman's spiritual motherhood. In this event the patroness of culture becomes its squanderer. By comparison the pleasure-loving woman of recent times is relatively harmless. Herself in possession of the advantages of culture, fostering them almost to the point of worship without rendering them fruitful or sharing them with others, this type of woman is in a measure sister to the selfish mother who wants her child for herself alone. Such an attitude indicates a lack of reverence for the purposes of culture, although not as yet for culture in itself.

Just as a woman in descending from her womanliness loses her sense of motherhood, so also in declining from her cultural level she loses her appreciation of that which really requires care and solace. She then shows an inclination to become loud, strident, ultrasophisticated. This tendency is the form peculiar to woman when she loses her standards of cultural evaluation. There is a fine but extremely significant line from that which is originally unimportant, overlooked, misunderstood, or even opposed, leading up to the very height of culture, that is, from out of time into timelessness. A glance at the history of great men and their lifework will demonstrate the agreement that exists largely between this line of contemporary ascent and their destinies, indicating the more conclusively that the enduring does not and cannot depend upon the momentary. Of this the life stories of geniuses like Hebbel, Nietzsche, Richard Wagner serve as examples. They are instances also of the cultural significance of the maternal woman. She who is timeless is related to that which is beyond time.

However, she is related also to that which is eternal, for in the last resort the import of all culture points to that which is beyond it. The role of the motherly woman as its protectress is fully realized only in her role as the guardian of religious values, and becomes thoroughly understandable only through the position of the mother in the religious realm.

In motherhood as nature has fashioned it, life and death rest side by side. The stream of generations breaks forth out of eternity, and there also it empties itself. Endlessness is the earthly sister of eternity. The Berceuse of the Breton saga who whispers into the ears of perishing sailors the songs that she heard their mothers sing, finds a profound interpretation in the novel *Ida Elisabeth*, through the death of little Sölvi. In describing the feelings of the mother of the dying child, Sigrid Undset writes, "It seemed to her as though she had lived through this before, when giving birth, at the moment when the child came forth from her and a wave from out of some titanic, endless sea washed over her, tearing something away. But after the wave rolled back again, a whimpering, quivering little being lay beside her, as though they both had been thrown ashore. The same breaker from out of an invisible eternity was now passing over her, and the wild, rending woe that she felt before in her body, was trifling in comparison with that which was tearing her today. The surf receded; but this time it had carried Sölvi away."

The surf that breaks forth out of eternity and rolls back to eternity opens the mother's womb, as it were, in the hour of birth like a portal leading two ways: the life that comes out of an invisible eternity enters the visible world of time. From eternity to eternity, expressed in religious terms, means from God to God.

Having acquired this knowledge we shall leave *Ida Elisabeth*. That such an understanding of the nature of woman's universal motherhood should be gained from a realization of the very essence of motherhood proves the imaginative power of this novel; above all, its gripping conclusiveness. It shows by literary means, as it were, what is meant in theology when we say that nature constitutes the prerequisite of grace, that grace functions everywhere, not in contradiction, but in correspondence with and as a continuation of the ascending plane of nature. *Ida Elisabeth*, therefore, leads us only to the door of the Church where the figure of another woman awaits us, Sigrid Undset's *Kristin Lavrandsdatter*.

The significance of this tremendous novel which stands at the threshold of a time of spiritual upheaval that is still of immeasurable proportions, constitutes an awareness of this very upheaval on the part of woman. The symptomatic meaning of this great book is that here a woman with all her powers, with all the forces of a full-blooded, unbroken womanliness and motherliness, is made to confront our epoch, uprooted as it is, in so far as the orientation toward nature is concerned. This woman is at the same time the counterthrust against the flightiness of the age in respect to religion. The first two volumes, *The Bridal Wreath* and *The Mistress of Husaby*, are filled with the storming primeval strength of Northern blood and destiny; but the third volume has *The Cross* as subtitle. Along the way of Kristin, who becomes a Christian, we witness the entire evolution from the natural experience of womanhood and motherhood to the new phase of a motherhood conceived in a Christian spirit. Kristin comes to the Church; but the Church approaches her through her nature, for it is precisely from the union between nature and the life of a mother that she fashions the points of contact with the religious destiny of woman and mother.

The Church also respects woman in her natural capacity of mother. The nuptial Mass is filled with the promise of the blessings of children: "May you see the children of your children!" In physical motherhood the Church beholds the original and primal destiny of woman, and sees in her the mother of people and of nations. In a magnificent vision, the prayers with which she supports her as she faces her difficult hour reach out far beyond individual life: "O may all peoples praise you! May the races be glad and rejoice, for the land is giving forth its fruit!" This is just one brief text taken from the nuptial Mass liturgy. At the moment when the woman withdraws into the deepest concealment, the Church intones over her the great hymn of all peoples, and makes of her who is mute with pain, one who praises God the Creator. In the consecration of a queen, the Church proclaims the same thought, while she anoints her below the heart where she is to carry the child.

The heroic concept of motherhood on the part of the Church is in line with her view of woman as the mother of the people. As she blesses the woman upon her entering marriage, only as the one who gives herself away unreservedly and promises to be true to one man for life, for better or for worse, so the Church also expects of a mother that she give her whole life to the child. The ethical standards of the Church, then, are much more heroic than those of secularism. Within the precincts of the Church the laws of nature, therefore, appear to be preserved in full, while modern society, as we noticed before, widely ignores the dangers that arise when these laws are disregarded.

The undelivered child in its mother's womb is in a twofold sense unredeemed. As the mother must bring it physically into the world so the Church gives it supernatural life; for the Church also represents a maternal category, so to speak, in the spiritual and religious sense. When she prays over the woman, who in suffering and in danger of death is about to give birth to a living child, two mothers are face to face with each other. For both know that life in itself, the unending recurrence of conception and birth, is not a final value, that ultimate value and meaning arise only from out of a higher life.

The higher life, which the Church has in mind when she applies strict standards in conformity with the law of nature, is reflected in nature itself as shown by the innate tendency to preserve a newly born being, if necessary at the expense of one already developed. To a mother this means that she will die rather than give up the child. As a mother the Church voices the sentiments of every mother creature, not only those of the human mother. The dominant heroic motif of the defense of the child thus is linked with the decisive hour of its entry into life, clearly identified with the overpowering natural urge which reaches deeply below the level of the human race, as for instance in the case of the lioness who wildly and yet movingly defends her cub. Thus, contrary to all objections of an intellectual or emotional kind, the attitude of the Church in regard to the mother is but a raising of the motherly instinct to a higher than the merely natural level by interpreting it as an obligation to be accepted consciously and absolutely.

All this explains why the Church has not accorded the mother the distinction of a special consecration such as the virgin and the bride receive. Compared to the consecration of a virgin or even to the sacrament of matrimony, the blessing given to the woman who is to become a mother, and the churching of the mother after the birth of the child, amount to a blessing such as one might pronounce over a budding meadowland. In the mind of the Church the earthly birth is but a first step. This apparent lack of estimation of the mother but accentuates her actual dignity because it is an attitude signifying the utter humility of nature in its complete surrender, of nature desiring nothing but to be simply nature, yet by this very attitude rising above itself to the level of the words of the Magnificat: "He hath exalted the humble."

Nature can be wild, but she is never willful; she may rear up with pain, but never with pride. Even in savagery, even in pain, nature fulfills the law of the Creator. The spirit, however, must still be conquered by Him. The motherly woman who surrenders to the forces of nature even as far as accepting death in order to give life to her child, by this very surrender, by this complete submersion in nature, portrays a part of the humility that nature possesses. The mother, in giving earthly life to the child, gives with it the prerequisite of redemption. Again, nature is the essential foundation of grace.

With this theological principle the concept of the defense of the child touches bedrock. The blessing and the curse once pronounced upon woman echo as from primeval times. The

88

prophecy that she shall bring forth her children in pain and the promise of the Woman who shall crush the serpent's head stand in closest relationship. The meaning of nature as the preliminary element of grace is clearly indicated by the presentation for supernatural birth of the child that has been born.

With this we may approach the great sacrament which is most intimately related to maternal life. It is not for the mother, however, but for the child. Baptism is the child's second, its supernatural birth, and the womb of the Church that receives it is the mother womb of its higher life. For the earthly mother the lovely analogy with the field that bears a blessing remains. This blessing rests upon the field, but is meant primarily for the fruit, and the bread that comes from the wheat is destined to become the carrier on the altar of the Body of our Lord. In the presence of the supernatural mother, the earthly mother recedes into the background. Because of the wish of the Church that the child be baptized as soon as possible, the attendance of the mother is in most instances impossible. This is profoundly symbolic, inasmuch as the mother gives evidence again of her being tied by nature, and her natural function representing but the first step to the supernatural birth of the child. Therefore not she but the sponsor assumes vicariously the duties of religious motherhood that belong to the Church.

Again, however, in this seemingly neglected position, the glorious outlines of the mother come forth the more distinctly. Just as the Church exalted the natural maternal instinct in proclaiming her specific duty to protect her child, so here also she applies a religious accent to the mother's natural unselfishness. With the offering of the child to God, the mother's destiny in its deepest sense is also given to God. The mother of the baptized child is the mother as daughter of the Church. Like her own child, she too was once presented by her mother to God. Together, as bound by a profound union of destinies, both Church and mother intone the *Magnificat*, that triumphal song of the mercy that is "from generation to generation."

89

The second birth of the child is accomplished in its religious education. The woman, who as the physical mother stands for a part of nature, represents as a Christian mother a portion of the Church. In the religious training of the child, the Church acts through the mother as through one of her members, while the mother functions consciously as a member of the Church. This means that from the mother of the baptized child a light spreads once more upon nature as the preliminary step toward grace. For the mother the natural process of expecting the child repeats itself as a spiritual process. Again the same stream of life circulates through mother and child; but instead of the shared physical space they have entered a spiritual area, and the forces of blood have given place to the powers of the spirit.

Again the woman is expectant. The very nature of this expectancy implies that the child she is awaiting is not actually formed by her, but from her. At the moment of conception she did not take it, but received it; therefore she could not consciously fashion it according to her own wishes. She could carry only that which was confided to her, placing her strength at the disposal of the child, while allowing this strength to be used. That which held good in the physical development of the child is true also of its spiritual growth. The attitude of the Christian mother remains that of the expectant one. As in the physical realm, so in bringing up her child she cannot fashion it according to her own wishes; she can only foster and protect that which was entrusted to her. This, in its religious sense, means the divine image in the growing human being. The child that in the natural sense the mother conceived by its father is in the religious sense the child of the Creator. He creates; she co-operates, with reverence. If the disposition of nature as the preliminary condition of grace revealed itself in the physical mother, then this disposition becomes manifest from the viewpoint of the Christian mother as the co-operation of the creature with divine creation.

In the light of this fact, the great theme of the Marian dogma refers also to the maternal woman. The co-operating creature is the daughter of the Eternal Woman, the reflected carrier of the *Fiat mihi*. If the attitude of the Christian mother toward her child is derived from its character as a child of God, her bearing toward her own maternal destiny is inspired by the life of Mary.

The Christian interpretation of the life of a mother rises up in three steps, corresponding to the three phases of the rosary prayer in its joyful, sorrowful, and glorious mysteries. As this great, popular, and at the same time highly contemplative prayer represents praying to Mary as Mother, so it likewise betokens the specific prayer of the mother. It is the chain of beads that links the life of the Christian mother to that of the Eternal Mother. In this threefold prayer the praying woman encompasses the mysteries of her own motherhood, that through the mystery of the Mother of all mothers they may be glorified. The earthly mother also has received her child from God; as His gift she has carried it and given it birth. Like Mary, she has presented it to God in the temple, and like her she has found it again in the temple.

While the joyful mysteries contemplate the life proper to the Mother, the sorrowful mysteries consider only the life of the Son. They make no mention of the Mother; for she lives in her Child, and His sufferings are enclosed within her life as the sorrowful mysteries are included in the *Ave Maria*. As the mother could not of her own power fashion either the body or the soul of her child, so she is likewise unable to determine its destiny. The child comes into life; she but cherishes it, which means that sooner or later it will progress beyond the mother. It must progress beyond her. As every life is independent as an existence, so also it is independent as a mission.

The mother lives in the child, but the child does not live in the mother. Every mother's destiny is, in the last analysis, the unending renewal of the pangs of giving birth. To give life to a child means in the last resort that the child detaches itself from her life. In the anguish of birth only the first stage of this process is accomplished. For every mother, sooner or later the hour comes when she, like Mary, must seek her child, sorrowing; and another, a heavier hour comes when the child may say: "What have I to do with you?" The Island of Riches of which Ruth Schaumann writes in her book, Yves, by which she designates that blessed solitude of mother and child, usually becomes for the mother at a certain time of her life an island of painful loneliness. There is no loneliness on earth like that of a mother; she is not being parted from some other loved one, but the sword that pierces her heart separates her from her own flesh and blood.

Sooner or later, concealed or unconcealed, the image of the Sorrowful Mother, the Pietà, appears over the life of every mother. In the book of destiny the designations of the sorrows of mothers are manifold. They include the suffering over the child that by a necessity of nature must go its own way, down to the estrangement between the generations, even to the complete loss of the child through misfortune, guilt, or death. Under the religious aspect all these griefs of the mother have but one name, the name by which Sigrid Undset entitled the third volume of her great novel. It is The Cross. Kristin Lavransdatter, who sacrificed for her children even her relationship to a loved husband, ends in complete estrangement from her older children. Her youngest and dearest child dies, while she herself dies for a strange child. With this conclusion the whole pathway of the sorrowful mother is traversed.

The rending of a child from its mother comes about most radically through death. Then, in the presence of a mother's love the Cross arises so strongly that it cannot be ignored. It is in the death of the child, however, that the detachment of the child from its mother appears in its true religious significance. Like a falling light this meaning plunges in the face of death through all the various phases of maternal tragedy. As Mary's sorrow was fundamentally determined by the work of Redemption on the part of her divine Son, so the most profound interpretation of every maternal sorrow is associated with the child's destiny for God. The Son who was presented in the Temple is in effect already the One who died on the cross, but He who dies on the cross remains also the One who was found in the Temple. As the second last decade of the joyful mysteries points toward the sorrowful mysteries, so likewise the last decade of the sorrowful rosary swings back, as it were, into the joyful. It really swings beyond it, for the glorious mysteries mean transfiguration. The Son, ascended into heaven, draws His Mother after Him. The unloosing of the child from its mother, understood in its ultimate religious significance as the destination of the child for God, implies in God the final, the indissoluble union.

This union is twofold. The ascended Christ, who drew His Mother into heaven to be with Him, is also the Christ who continues to dwell upon earth, and to Mary's life of glory corresponds her life in the Church. With the words from the cross: "Behold thy Mother, behold thy son," the dying Savior summons the disciple to be Mary's spiritual son, and Mary to be the spiritual mother of the disciple. St. John stands for the Apostles in general, and all those whom the disciples of the Lord baptize for Christ are also the children of Mary. In that hour when her life as Mother of Christ seems fully concluded, she becomes in truth the universal Mother of Christians.

For the second time the words of the *Magnificat* are fulfilled: "And all generations shall call me blessed!" The Gospel does not speak of Mary again; but the Acts of the Apostles show her to us, much as the great religious art of the Christian West has painted her: with the Apostles in Jerusalem, awaiting the coming of the Holy Spirit. As the words of the *Magnificat* became a reality a second time in Mary when she stood beneath the cross, so on the morning of Pentecost for the second time the Holy Spirit descends upon her, and the Mother of Christ becomes the great Mother figure of Holy Mother the Church.

For the individual woman as a daughter of Mary this means

that in the Church, by reason of her religious mission, her apostolate as mother, the woman has her place beside the bearer of religious fatherhood, beside the priesthood of the man which gives spiritual life. Only in this apostolate are Christ's words: "Whoever receives one such little child in My name receiveth Me," fulfilled for the woman, not only in their transcendental but also in their actual sense. The life of the Church as religious life is the life of Christ growing within the human soul. As the global form of the earth, uplifted into a sacred symbol, appears in the cupola of a cathedral, so at this point the religious concept assumes the primal form in order to elevate and transfigure it. We have seen the compassionate love of the maternal woman extend itself into a universal motherliness, because of her own child's need of care and protection. We see this universal motherhood uplifted by religious vocation into the service of Christ growing within the souls of men. The radiance from the crown of the Mother of Mercy parallels the radiance from the crown of the Mother of Divine Grace.

The woman as mother was not made the subject of a special act of consecration, nor does her apostolate receive this distinction. It is but a part of the Lay Apostolate in which every Christian may participate. The mother never reaches her goal in being mother, but her goal is the child. The Great Sacrament rests upon the Son of the Mother, not upon the Mother herself; but by this very fact the mission of woman in the Church is linked closely with the essential quality of the Church herself. Because of this fact she represents a basic aspect of the very essence of the Church. In her character as mother the Church is a co-operating principle; the One who works within her is Christ Himself.

This no doubt is one reason why the Church could never entrust the priesthood to woman. It is the same reason that determined St. Paul's ruling that the woman be veiled when attending religious services. The priesthood could not be confided to woman, for thereby the very meaning of woman in the Church would have been eliminated. A part of the essential nature of the Church of which woman is the symbol would have been annihilated. St. Paul's command was not prompted by customs prevailing in his day, but it actually is a demand of the timeless Church upon woman who, in her religious significance, is timeless woman.

Like natural birth, religious birth is profoundly concealed. The Church also can say of herself what God disclosed to Moses, namely, that He would allow all His glory to pass over him and let him preach the Name of the Lord; that to whomever He is gracious, He is gracious; and upon whomever He has mercy, He has mercy; but that no one may look upon His countenance. The essentially spiritual life of the Church is hidden; hence, the inevitable error of judgment on the part of those who venture to size up and even criticize the religious life of the Church from without. This is an absurdity comparable only to that of demanding of the surgeon that his dissecting knife locate the soul within the body.

We have said that woman, by her apostolate as mother, comes into a most intimate relationship with the inner life of the Church. She does this by means of her own hidden nature, for in the Church the apostolate of woman is first of all one of silence; and it is in the innermost enclosure of the sacred realm that the religious character of woman necessarily carries its strongest emphasis. The apostolate of silence means that woman is called upon above all to represent the hidden life of Christ in the Church. Therefore, as the bearer of her religious mission, she is the daughter of Mary.

This intimates the maternal apostolate of woman in its ultimate depth. Only a time like that of the recent past, which often has failed both in a religious and in a natural sense, could conclude from this apostolate that it meant underrating woman. One could never dare to take a stand against this mistake with the feeble assurance that here and there woman had labored and spoken within the Church, for she has never done so within the sacred precincts of the priesthood. The direct charismatic vocation, which in individual cases as in that of St. Catherine of Siena has broken woman's silence in the Church, is realized only in extraordinary situations, never in the line of the predominant order.

In relation to this thought, we come upon an extraordinary piece of writing. In The Tidings Brought to Mary, Paul Claudel describes with a depth that is almost overwhelming the significance of woman in the Church. His writings differ from all other contemporary poetry and dramatic art, in fact from nearly all the writings of the past few centuries, not only because they are inspired by generally Christian and religious thinking, but because they are entirely in line with the dogma of the Church. This explains the unique sublimity that is characteristic of Paul Claudel; this too is the cause of his extreme loneliness.

Under the symbol of the awakening of Mara's dead child through Violaine, the leper, The Tidings Brought to Mary portrays the birth of life as coming from the utmost depths of religious experience. Violaine, the broken vessel of the sacrifice, is made worthy of this birth after having offered to God the surrender of her entire life, and having accepted the terrible disease which means becoming an outcast of society. According to Claudel, the man is the active power in the Church. "O God, I thank You for having created me a father of churches," says the architect, Pierre de Craon. "Man is the priest; but woman's privilege is to sacrifice herself." In these words the mystery of religious motherhood is related to the priestly mystery of the Consecration. Violaine's miracle, while at first it remains hidden, yet transforms, we might almost say transubstantiates, everything. The dark eyes of the awakened child take on light such as there was in the eyes of Violaine before her illness; but Mara, the selfish one, from whom the child inherited her black eyes, finds forgiveness at last in that she may be a sister to Violaine. Souls are transformed, "transubstantiated." Violaine's miracle happens in the blessed night of Christmas.

Always and everywhere, contact with the Church means participation in her universality. Beneath the cross where Mary became the spiritual Mother of all Christians, stands not only the woman who has offered her own child to God, but also the woman who has sacrificed to God the wish or the hope for a child of her own, or who was willing to give a child to God. The mother of Christ who is born in a human soul, is the mother who folds the hands of her child in its first prayer; it is also the nun who lovingly gives support to her spiritual daughters on the heights of the religious life. It is Monica, the great saint of mothers, who by her prayers gave life to her son a second time and made Augustine a saint. It is also the virginal saint, Catherine of Siena, as *dolcissima mamma*, "sweetest mother" to her spiritual son. It is even the lonely woman upon her sickbed who can but experience the birth of Christ within her own soul.

Contact with the Church, as we indicated above, always implies universality. Here, in the religious sphere, the mother becomes the all-inclusive form of woman's life, in fact the absolute form. This absolute position in which the Church places the mother means that the all-embracing form of motherhood, because it is all embracing, also includes the virgin. Upon the summit of the religious mission of woman, the conclusion swings back to the beginning. Over the timeless woman the image of the Eternal Woman appears. The religious mother concept of the Church is indissolubly bound to her who as Virgin is Mother and as Mother is Virgin.

Against this background the tremendous meaning of the dogma for every individual woman's life unfolds once more. The all-embracing form implies also the all-encompassing task. For the woman who prays, the contemplative prayer of the rosary represents her own life reflected in the life of Mary. The rosary, as the great mother prayer to a Mother, introduces every individual maternal mystery of Mary with the invocation of the Virgin. Every such invocation, however, is followed by the contemplation of a mystery of motherhood. There actually is a constant link-up in the rosary between the mystery of motherhood and the one of virginity.

The interpenetration of these two mysteries when expressed in the sorrowful rosary, explains the unutterable impression of Michelangelo's Pietà. In the startling youthfulness of Mary, who in her final agony renders her dead Son back to God, the gentle Virgin of the *Fiat mihi* — "Be it done unto me" — appears again. The mysteries of the Virgin and the Mother become interrelated again in the joyful decades. Here their image is represented in Tiepolo's painting of St. Rose of Lima to whom the Madonna is presenting to the Christ Child.

* * *

After all this is said we may now by way of conclusion gain a comprehensive view of the image of the Christian woman. The Christian woman is not woman as such, but she is woman placed in an order of life ordained by God. Every stage of this life denotes a complete and independent fulfillment, but also a bond of union with the collective and primal image of woman's life. The life of every woman is immediately concerned with the unfolding of this image, with the partial representation as virgin or mother. But at the last it is a matter of the reconstruction of the eternal image. The virgin must absorb the concept of spiritual motherhood, while the mother must time and again return to a spiritual virginity. Upon the success of this interchange the well-being of every woman depends, as also does the victory over what may be the tragedy of the virgin or that of the mother.

This means nothing other than that the salvation of every individual woman is indissolubly bound not only to the image of Mary, but also to Mary's mission. The conscious reproduction of the eternal image is possible for the individual woman only in the attitude of handmaid of the Lord, in the constant readiness of her surrender to God. The involuntary confirmation of this absolute meaning and requirement on the part of the eternal image, however, extends far down into the secular life. Even aside from a woman's Christian obligation, the balance proper to her life, the overcoming of its tragic elements whether in the virginal or the maternal state, can always be accomplished only through an approach, albeit unconscious, toward the reproduction of the eternal image.

Mary does not signify only the salvation of the woman, but also salvation through the woman. If it is the individual woman's concern to reproduce this eternal image in her life, its restoration must also be the concern of the world. Violaine's sickness, in Claudel's story, is related to original sin. "O Violaine, O woman through whom the temptation came!" Pierre de Craon cries out. This illness, however, is also related to the special sin of the times. The book is permeated with the apocalyptic atmosphere of our own day, but mirrored in the closing medieval period which in its chaotic disorder approached but did not equal our times.

The rebirth of the dead child completely transforms the souls of those concerned and, through them, also the world. When, on the same Christmas night during which Violaine's miracle takes place, a renewal in the secular order begins, it is but the reflection of this inner transformation. The king, who puts an end to the state of confusion in his country, is led to coronation by St. Joan, Violaine's spiritual sister. The birth from out of the depth of religious life is, at the final issue, the new birth of life itself. For this reason, in Christian countries, our ancestors placed Mary's image not only over the entrance to their churches, but also over the doors of their homes, their town halls, and market places.

What Pierre de Craon says of the martyr, Justitia, is true of Violaine as it is of St. Joan: "She too was only a modest little girl until God summoned her to openly avow her vocation." As they both come out of obscurity, so into obscurity they return. Violaine opens the way for Pierre de Craon. He strides out into the world of great undertakings, while she disappears under the veil of the leper, as St. Joan does under the veil of the funeral pyre. Pierre, the "father of churches," builds the cathedral whose mighty vaults "rest on the cornerstone of Justitia's tender remains." Joan's work, however, is completed by the men of her people. She too but opened the way for them. The salvation that woman brings always points far beyond her; its proper fulfillment, its success upon earth, is man's appointed mission.

And now the last of the three great forms of woman's life reappears, that while it reflects the eternal image, it may also become part of that image. Mary as Virgin Mother is likewise the spouse of the Holy Spirit. Again the dominant paths of woman's life intersect. Violaine, who as a virgin represents the image of the mother, stands at the same time upon the double line of the Christian spouse. It is the child of the man whom she loves and who at one time was destined to be her husband, that she restores to life; but she does it as the spouse of Christ.

As the renewal of culture depends on whether the other half of being, the woman's countenance, becomes visible again in the face of the creative man, so the true salvation of the world depends on whether Mary's features grow visible also in his face. The announcement made to Mary is fundamentally an annunciation to the whole human race. The bride who in the presence of man represents the virgin and the mother, represents also the Virgin Mother; she represents, in fact, the Marian influence in the life and work of man, and she does it as the half part of his own being.

With this we have come to the final consideration. Woman's mission, reaching out far beyond the woman herself, touches upon the mystery of the world. The Annunciation to Mary is a message to every creature, but to the creature as represented in Mary. The renewal of the eternal image through the Marian mission of the woman completes itself in the vicarious role of her who represents the creature. Mary stands for her daughters, but her daughters must also stand for her. In Claudel's poetry the apocalyptic line leads over to the atmosphere of Advent.

There is Advent until the coming of Christ on Judgment Day! But time and again the Annunciation to Mary precedes the fulfillment through Christ, vision follows upon concealment, as Redemption does upon the humility of surrender; as the unfolding of heaven upon a willing acceptance, upon the "Fiat" of the creature.